Simulations in Swift 5

Design and Implement with Swift Playgrounds

Beau Nouvelle

Apress®

Simulations in Swift 5: Design and Implement with Swift Playgrounds

Beau Nouvelle
Victoria, Australia

ISBN-13 (pbk): 978-1-4842-5336-6   ISBN-13 (electronic): 978-1-4842-5337-3
https://doi.org/10.1007/978-1-4842-5337-3

Managing Director, Apress Media LLC: WelmoedSpahr
Acquisitions Editor: Aaron Black
Development Editor: James Markham
Coordinating Editor: Jessica Vakili

Distributed to the book trade worldwide by Springer Science+Business Media New York, 233 Spring Street, 6th Floor, New York, NY 10013. Phone 1-800-SPRINGER, fax (201) 348-4505, e-mail orders-ny@springer-sbm.com, or visit www.springeronline.com. Apress Media, LLC is a California LLC and the sole member (owner) is Springer Science + Business Media Finance Inc (SSBM Finance Inc). SSBM Finance Inc is a **Delaware** corporation.

For information on translations, please e-mail rights@apress.com, or visit http://www. apress.com/rights-permissions.

Apress titles may be purchased in bulk for academic, corporate, or promotional use. eBook versions and licenses are also available for most titles. For more information, reference our Print and eBook Bulk Sales web page at http://www.apress.com/bulk-sales.

Any source code or other supplementary material referenced by the author in this book is available to readers on GitHub via the book's product page, located at www.apress.com/ 978-1-4842-5336-6. For more detailed information, please visit http://www.apress.com/ source-code.

Printed on acid-free paper

For Elle, Harkoa, and Maple

Table of Contents

About the Author

Beau Nouvelle has been developing iOS applications for over 8 years. He has contracted for companies like IBM as well as industrious start-ups. He also enjoys fun side projects in coding, such as generating artwork, creating virtual civilizations, and tweaking values here and there to see how things turn out. Beau loves to use computers to bridge art and math together and fill in missing skills. No one ever set out to create a particular fractal, it's the numbers that do that.

About the Technical Reviewer

Jason Whitehorn is an experienced entrepreneur and software developer and has helped many oil and gas companies automate and enhance their oilfield solutions through field data capture, SCADA, and machine learning. Jason obtained his Bachelor of Science in Computer Science from Arkansas State University, but he traces his passion for development back many years before then, having first taught himself to program BASIC on his family's computer while still in middle school.

When he's not mentoring and helping his team at work, writing, or pursuing one of his many side projects, Jason enjoys spending time with his wife and four children and living in the Tulsa, Oklahoma, region. More information about Jason can be found on his web site: `https://jason.whitehorn.us`.

CHAPTER 1

Swift Playgrounds

We're going to be creating most of our projects with Xcode's Swift Playgrounds. They're the easiest and fastest way to start writing Swift. I use them all the time for prototyping, or working through math problems and refining algorithms. Once I'm happy with the code, I will usually move it into a more significant project.

Playgrounds will run automatically. You can type a line of code, and the results will appear immediately. It makes for a rapid feedback loop, where you can iterate quickly on your project, find mistakes sooner, and stay productive. Larger Xcode projects, like the ones used for full applications, can take minutes to compile and launch in a simulator. Playgrounds help to reduce the wait times between writing code and testing.

If you're already familiar with playgrounds and already have Xcode installed, you can skip this chapter.

System Requirements

At the time of writing, the latest release version of Xcode is 11 and Swift 5.1. There has been some major progress with Swift since version 4.0, which is what the first edition of this book was based on. For one thing, we now have something called ABI (Application Binary Interface) stability. This feature provides source compatibility between different versions of Swift moving forward. So if you bought this book and the latest version of Swift is 6.0, don't worry as all exercises should still work.

© Beau Nouvelle 2019
B. Nouvelle, *Simulations in Swift 5*, https://doi.org/10.1007/978-1-4842-5337-3_1

Up until ABI stability, there could be significant breaking changes between different versions of Swift. This would require developers to rebuild their dependencies and refactor any code that would no longer compile.

Another added benefit is that developers will no longer need to embed a version of the Swift standard library within their apps. This means that shipped Swift apps will take up less space on a user's device. However, since this book's exercises are all within Xcode's Swift Playgrounds, shipping code isn't something we'll need to worry about.

You'll need

1. macOS 10.15 or later

2. At least 15GB of free space

Playgrounds run well on most hardware; however, if you plan on developing larger projects, I recommend that you have a Mac built within the last 4 years with a built-in SSD. Xcode's Interface Builder tends to get overwhelmed with just a few view controllers on the best of hardware, and compile times on 5200rpm drives can be frustratingly slow.

Installation

The installation will take some time on slower connections. The download size is about 6GB.

You can also install Swift on Linux machines, but that process is out of scope for this book.

1. Open the App Store on your Mac.

2. Search for "Xcode".

3. Click Xcode within the search results to navigate to its store page (see Figure 1-1).

4. Install. It's free!

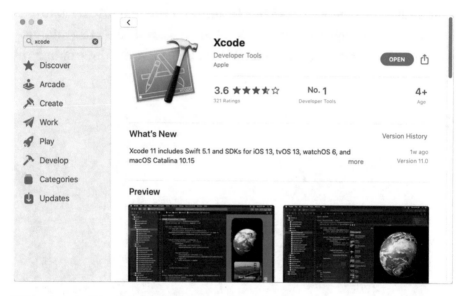

Figure 1-1. *Xcode's store page in the App Store app*

If you don't own a Mac or have an Internet connection that allows you to download 6GB of data, there are some web sites out there that allow you to write and compile Swift directly in the browser. The *IBM Swift Sandbox* is one such web site. This will do fine for a few early projects in the book, but later on we'll be using the live views feature of Xcode's playgrounds to render some artwork and watch our simulations come to life.

Your First Project

After installation, you can find Xcode in the applications folder on your Mac. When first opening Xcode, it will ask you for permission to install some additional components. Click **Install**, and you may also need to enter your Mac's login password to continue. This will take a few minutes to complete. On the start-up screen (Figure 1-2), there are three options on the left.

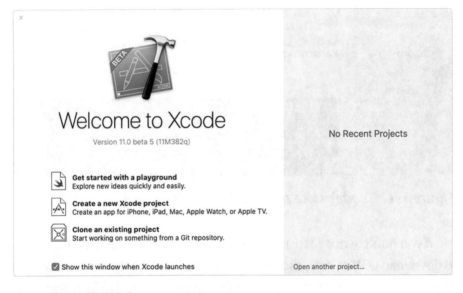

Figure 1-2. *Xcode's start-up screen*

Get started with a playground, Create a new Xcode project, and **Clone an existing project**. We're going to click the top one; **Get started with a playground**.

On the following screen (Figure 1-3), ensure that **iOS** is highlighted in the tab bar at the top, select the blank project template, and click **Next**.

Figure 1-3. *Template selection screen*

Now you'll be asked to make a decision on where you would like to save this playground. I have a dedicated development folder within my documents for projects like these. This is a great place to put your projects if you want to ensure that you have a backup and access to them on all of your Apple devices. This is all handled for you; anything you put into the documents folder will be sent to iCloud storage.

Once you've done that, click **Create**!

The Code Editor

That large area with the text `"Hello, playground"` is where you'll write your code, but before we do that, let's have a little look around first.

The bar at the top of the window displays status information for your project (Figure 1-4). This is usually for things like the current build status, or if Xcode has detected any errors.

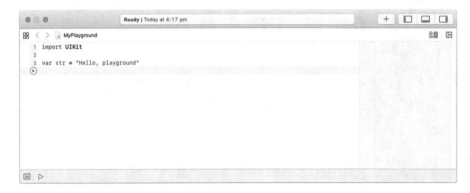

Figure 1-4. *New playground project window*

To the right of the status bar is a button with a plus symbol; clicking this will open up a snippets window. Snippets are usually small blocks of reusable code, but they can be any size really. This is a great time-saving feature, especially if you find yourself writing the same code often. Clicking and holding on this button will open up a mini menu which allows you to also choose to open the media library. The media library will be empty. We won't be using either of these features in this book.

The last three tab buttons relate to some extra panels you can show and hide on the left, bottom, and right side of the edit window. The first button opens up the navigator, and in the navigator you can switch between the files that make up your project. The middle button shows the debug area—which we'll look at in depth in a moment—and the right one will toggle the inspector panel. We won't be using the inspector panel, but we will be making use of the other two.

At the bottom left of the playground window, there should be a play button. Click and hold until a little dropdown window appears and ensure that **Automatically Run** is selected.

Go ahead and delete "Hello, playground". The playground should auto-run, and after a second or two you'll get an error, the debug area will open, and the line of code in the editor causing the issue will be highlighted in red (Figure 1-5).

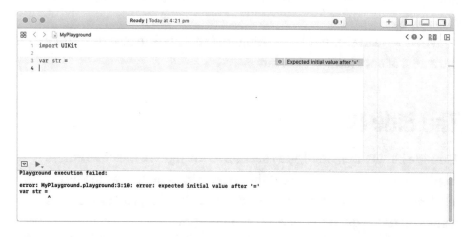

Figure 1-5. *Playground window showing debug area with an error*

If the debug area does not open automatically for you, double-check that you have auto-run turned on.

The Debug Area

Since the error is indicating that our variable str is missing an initial value, let's write some code to fix this by typing "Hello," followed by your name.

```
var str = "Hello, Name"
```

After you're done, the playground will auto-run again, and the error printout should disappear from the debug area, and you will see a result in the side bar.

Below this line add a print function:

```
print(str)
```

The print() function will print out anything you pass in as a parameter, to the debug area. After the playground runs again, you will now see the text "Hello, <yourname>" printed out where the error was previously.

We'll be using print() all throughout this book to give us feedback on the status of our running simulations.

The Side Bar

The side bar is the shaded/gray section to the right of the code editor. It displays contextual results from the code written on the same line on the left. This content can be a number of things. Strings, print statements, results of math equations, or even a loop count.

Clicking on the little square to the right of the text will show the result directly inside the code editor. This feature isn't all that useful if your result is only plain text; however, it's super powerful for viewing outputs that are drawn. Such as images and graphs.

In some cases, the playground will generate a graph for you automatically. This can usually be triggered by changing a property's value many times over the course of the program. I'll show you what I mean a little later in this book.

Themes

One last thing. If you're like me, and most other developers in the world, you probably prefer writing your code with darker themes to reduce eye strain. You can change the theme by going to **Xcode ➤ Preferences ➤ Fonts & Colours**. Even better, macOS also has a night mode and Xcode looks great with it turned on (see Figure 1-6).

Figure 1-6. *Playground window with dark theme applied and macOS darkmode turned on*

Summary

In this chapter we downloaded Xcode from the Mac App Store and learned how to create our first Swift playground. We also discovered some of the tools Xcode provides for us to make development easier, such as the debugger and information displayed in the side bar.

Even though we've only scratched the surface of what can be done with Xcode's Playgrounds, I think we're ready to move on to creating our first simulation. We'll dive deeper and learn as we go.

CHAPTER 2

The Monty Hall Problem

The Monty Hall Problem gets its name from a TV game show that originated in 1963 named *Let's Make a Deal*. The problem is a counterintuitive puzzle where you have the opportunity to choose from one of three closed doors. Two doors have a goat behind them, and one has a car. The aim is to pick a door with the car.

After you make a selection, instead of opening the door you chose, the host will open one of the remaining doors. Monty knows what's behind each door, so he always chooses one with a goat behind it. He then asks if you want to keep your original choice, or switch to the other closed door.

Many people will assume that with one door eliminated they now have a 50% chance of winning the car, so what they do next is irrelevant. Stick with the original choice or switch. It doesn't matter... or does it?

We're going to design a simulation that will run through the game a thousand times to find an answer to the question; Is it better to switch or stay?

© Beau Nouvelle 2019
B. Nouvelle, *Simulations in Swift 5*, https://doi.org/10.1007/978-1-4842-5337-3_2

Coding the Game

Create a new Swift playground and name it MontyHallProblem. We'll start out by creating a few properties at the top of the file. These properties will hold the values we'll need to make the simulation run.

```
let doors = ["🐐", "🐐", "🚗"]
let numberOfGames = 1000
var switchWins = 0
var stayWins = 0
```

The let keyword informs the compiler that we won't be changing the values stored here during the execution of our program. The var keyword indicates the opposite. While we could mark all properties as var, being explicit helps the compiler perform some optimizations and also makes it easier for future developers to read our code.

Prize	🐐	🐐	🚗
Door number	1	2	3
Array index	0	1	2

For our doors, we'll be using an array of three strings. A goat emoji ("🐐") indicates the presence of a goat, and a car emoji ("🚗") represents the car. You can pop open the emoji window by pressing the keyboard combo **control+command+space**. It even gives you a little search bar to help find the emoji you're looking for. If you don't want to use emoji, just replace them with "goat" and "car".

With numberOfGames set to 1000, the simulation will run 1000 times. This should produce plenty of data for us to determine the best strategy for winning.

Finally, we have two properties to help us keep track of our results; switchWins or staysWins will be incremented every time switching or staying on a door reveals the car.

Add a for-loop below this list of properties. The loop will execute any code placed inside it a thousand times.

```
for _ in 0..<numberOfGames {

}
```

We now have the main structure of our simulation laid out, but before we go any further, let's break each game into a few simple steps. Many programming tasks can seem really daunting at first, and it can be difficult to know where to start, or what solutions to begin trying out. By breaking larger tasks down into smaller ones, your problems become much easier to solve. What happens each game?

1. Choose a random door.

2. If the randomly chosen door is the car, increment stayWins by one. Otherwise, increment switchWins by one.

3. Repeat steps 1 and 2 for numberOfGames.

It's that simple. There's no need for us to reveal goats, or reshuffle the doors each game. We don't need to write code that actually decides on switching, and seeing what's behind the other door. We can make both choices at the same time for each game and record the results.

It might be easier to see this logic by thinking of playing the game with 100 doors instead of 3. Behind the doors there are 99 goats and 1 car. On the first try, the contestant has a 1% (1 in 100) chance of choosing correctly. After making the selection, the host will reveal 98 doors that contain goats and leave 1 hidden. Switching now gives the contestant a 99% chance of winning. Still don't believe me? We'll take a closer look at this scenario a little further on in the chapter.

There's no need to check every door within our program. There's no reason to play the host's part and remove doors from the game. Once the first selection is made, there is only one of two outcomes. Win, or lose. Stay, or switch.

On the other hand, if the host were to only reveal 1 other door of the remaining 99, our strategy would need to change. A programming challenge for another time perhaps?

For now, let's put this code between the curly braces of the for-loop.

```
let randomChoice = Int.random(in: 0..<doors.count)
let prize = doors[randomChoice]
if prize == "🚗" {
    stayWins += 1
} else {
    switchWins += 1
}
```

The first line uses `Int`'s built-in `random` function to generate an integer between 0 and `doors.count`. In our case, `doors.count` is 3. The `..<` operator means we want to include the numbers 0, 1, and 2. We need to include 0 because array indexes start at 0.

On the second line we pull a value from the `doors` array at the index `randomChoice`. So, if our random number generator were to give us a 1, our prize would be the 🐐 hidden behind door number 2.

Now that we have chosen our prize, all we need to do is check if it's the car. If that's the case we increment `stayWins` by 1. Otherwise, we increment `switchWins`.

Getting Results

The last thing to do here is to make our simulation generate some useful output for us to review. This code will be added after the closing curly brace of the for-loop.

```
print("Stay:", stayWins)
print("Switch:", switchWins)
```

If you don't see immediate results, you may have an error, or auto-run is turned off. Just a reminder, you can turn this back on by clicking and holding down the mouse button over the play arrow in the bottom left of the screen. Alternatively, you can stick to running your playgrounds manually, and just click play.

These are my results after running the simulation three times.

```
Stay: 337
Switch: 663
```

```
Stay: 353
Switch: 647
```

```
Stay: 328
Switch: 672
```

With any simulation like this, the greater the number of times it's run, the more accurate the results will be. However, set the number of games too high and you might be waiting a while for your results.

Here are the results of 1,000,000 games.

```
Stay: 333032
Switch: 666968
```

Running through a million games took roughly 30 seconds on my machine. With a sample size this high, I think we have enough data to make an assessment on the best strategy to increase our chances of winning the Monty Hall Problem. There's about a 66% chance of winning if the contestant decides to switch doors. So by running this simulation, we've learned that it's always better to make the switch when playing this game.

Improving Customization

The preceding implementation does the job well enough, but having more control over the input parameters would be better. The only thing we can really change at the moment is the number of games being played. Sure, we *could* add more doors to the array, but that would be incredibly time-consuming to write all that code if we wanted to see what a thousand-door simulation would look like.

Let's delete all that code and start fresh with a more flexible list of properties.

```
let numberOfDoors = 100
let numberOfGames = 1000
var switchWins = 0
var stayWins = 0
```

This time the array of doors has been replaced with an Int called numberOfDoors. We will use this to generate the doors array. numberOfGames is still set to 1000 and the scorekeeping variables also haven't changed.

Next, add this code below the properties we just created.

```
var doors = Array(repeating: "🐐", count: numberOfDoors)
let randomDoor = Int.random(in: 0..<doors.count)
doors[randomDoor] = "🚗"
```

Here we're initializing the doors array with 100 goats. On the next line we generate a random number between 0 and doors.count. The result will be an index where we'll put the car, which is what's happening in the final line of code. Now we have an array of doors with 99 🐐 and 1 🚗.

We can now use the same for-loop we created earlier to run games with these new starting conditions.

```
for _ in 0..<numberOfGames {
    let randomChoice = Int.random(in: 0..<doors.count)
    let prize = doors[randomChoice]
    if prize == "🚗" {
        stayWins += 1
    } else {
        switchWins += 1
    }
}
```

Let's review.

1. Generate an array of doors with a count of numberOfDoors with a 🐐 at each index.

2. Replace a random 🐐 with the 🚗.

3. Choose a random door.

4. If the randomly chosen door has a 🚗 behind it, increment stayWins by one. Otherwise, increment switchWins by one.

5. Repeat steps 3 and 4 for numberOfGames.

Slightly different this time, but the complexity hasn't changed all that much. Run your playground a few times and see what happens. Don't forget to put your logging statements back in!

```
print("Stay:", stayWins)
print("Switch:", switchWins)
```

These are my results from running the simulation three times.

```
Stay: 17
Switch: 983

Stay: 11
Switch: 989

Stay: 12
Switch: 988
```

This is exactly what we would expect. There's a 1 in 100 chance of winning the car by deciding to stick with the first choice. The more doors that are added to the game, the better the odds are of winning the car when making the switch.

We could experiment some more. We may want to change the number of doors chosen on the first pick, or the quantity of goats that are revealed. All kinds of parameters can be altered, added, or removed. Experimentation is where the real fun comes in with simulations.

Summary

Congratulations on having created your first simulation!

We learned a lot in this chapter about the Swift programming language including the let and var keywords, arrays, for-loops, and random number generation.

Something else I hope that you take away from this is to not always trust your intuition when it comes to matters of probability. Predictions can be wrong, and this is why we take the time to run experiments.

Before moving on to the next chapter, I urge you to have a play around with this simulation by changing a few values and seeing what results you get.

CHAPTER 3

Guessing Game

Here's a puzzle that features on Randall Munroe's XKCD blog, and is explained in the Numberphile YouTube video *"How to Win a Guessing Game."*

It works like this. Get a friend to pick two different real numbers without telling you what they are. They could roll a dice, generate them with a computer program or just imagine them. Have them write these numbers on two cards and place them facedown on a table. Your friend then chooses a card and flips it over. You now have to guess if the number written on the facedown card is larger or smaller than the one that is faceup.

So what are the odds of you guessing correctly? You can only select from two different answers. That gives you a 50% chance of winning this guessing game. Can we do better?

Let's find out.

Planning

As in the previous chapter, before we start writing any code, we need to break down our problem into easy-to-understand steps. Having things planned out first means fewer mistakes later.

© Beau Nouvelle 2019
B. Nouvelle, *Simulations in Swift 5*, https://doi.org/10.1007/978-1-4842-5337-3_3

1. Pick any two numbers. Most computer systems can work with 2^32 different values. So that's what we're going to be limited to in this simulation. From -2,147,483,648 to 2,147,483,647.

2. Reveal one of the numbers.

3. Make a guess.

At this point we're not thinking about how we can improve our odds. We just need to collect some results before we can do that. So, let's get a simple program together with the information we already know. Then we can refine our work and hopefully find a pattern that we can exploit to our advantage.

Coding the Game

Let's start out by creating a new playground and naming it GuessingGame. As always, we'll put out properties at the top of the file so that they're easier to discover and modify later.

```
let numberOfPuzzles = 1000
var numberOfCorrectGuesses = 0
```

Because we want to run the simulation a thousand times, we'll set numberOfPuzzles to 1000. We also need to keep track of how many times we made a correct guess. This property needs to be mutable. So, we've marked it with the var keyword and given it an initial value of 0.

Below this, create a loop using the numberOfPuzzles as the number of iterations.

```
for _ in 0..<numberOfPuzzles {
}
```

Referring to the list of steps we wrote earlier, the first thing we need to do inside this loop is generate two different numbers. These need to be random, and to keep it simple, I've chosen them to be numbers between 0 and 1,000,000, but we could use any range we wanted.

Put this code between the curly braces of the for-loop.

```
let firstNumber = Int.random(in: 0..<1_000_000)
let secondNumber = Int.random(in: 0..<1_000_000)
```

You can write integers in Swift using underscores _ as separators to make larger numbers easier to read. The compiler will interpret these numbers as if you had written them as 1000000.

Now we guess which of the two numbers is larger. One way to make a random guess between two numbers is to flip a coin. To do that we randomly generate a number between 0 and 100. We'll then reduce this number to a 0 or 1 (heads or tails) using the modulo operator. If the number is odd, we'll get a 1; if it's even (divisible by 2), we'll get a 0.

Put this line of code under the secondNumber declaration.

```
let coinFlip = Int.random(in: 0..<100) % 2
```

For this next part, let's say that if coinFlip has a value of 0, we'll guess that firstNumber is larger than secondNumber. Alternatively, if the result of the coin flip is a 1, we'll choose the second number to be the largest. If we guess correctly in either of the two cases, numberOfCorrectGuesses will increase by 1.

```
if coinFlip == 0 && firstNumber > secondNumber {
    numberOfCorrectGuesses += 1
} else if coinFlip == 0 && secondNumber > firstNumber {
    numberOfCorrectGuesses += 1
}
```

Outside the for-loop and at the bottom of the file, add a print statement so that we can see the results.

```
print("correctly guessed \(numberOfCorrectGuesses) times out of \(numberOfPuzzles)")
```

Run your playground a few times to check that everything is working correctly. You should be seeing an average output of around 500 correct guesses each time.

These results are what we expected to happen. There is a 50% chance to guess correctly. How are we going to improve on this?

Improving Our Chances

We're missing a crucial step. We even wrote it down during our planning phase. So far we've only accounted for steps 1 and 3. Pick two numbers, and guess which is higher.

We haven't done anything with revealing one of the numbers in our simulation. You might be wondering what good would this do? It seems like doing this wouldn't make any difference as it doesn't give you any information on the other number, but there must be a reason for why we get to see it. What can we possibly do with such information that would give us an advantage?

Let's try generating a third number to make some comparisons and see where that gets us.

Add a new property inside the for-loop under where we've declared secondNumber and call it myNumber.

```
let myNumber = Int.random(in: 0..<1_000_000)
```

In this experiment we'll see where myNumber sits in relation to the two other numbers. We'll also need a way to keep track of this. Again, at the top of the file, add three more properties.

```
var timesMyNumberIsLargest = 0
var timesMyNumberIsSmallest = 0
var timesMyNumberIsInBetween = 0
```

Inside the for-loop delete all code after let myNumber, including the coinFlip property, and add the following:

```
if myNumber >= max(firstNumber, secondNumber) {
    timesMyNumberIsLargest += 1
} else if myNumber <= min(firstNumber, secondNumber) {
    timesMyNumberIsSmallest += 1
} else {
    timesMyNumberIsInBetween += 1
}
```

Each time these conditions are met, we increment its respective variable.

The min() and max() functions take in two values and return the smallest, or largest of the two. This saves us from having to compare myNumber to both firstNumber and secondNumber individually.

Then after the closing curly brace of the for-loop, we'll print out the values to the debug console.

```
print("myNumber was largest \(timesMyNumberIsLargest) times.")
print("myNumber was smallest \(timesMyNumberIsSmallest) times.")
print("myNumber was in between \(timesMyNumberIsInBetween) times.")
```

Run the program a few times and take note of the results.

```
myNumber was largest 348 times.
myNumber was smallest 315 times.
myNumber was in between 337 times.
```

It's quite an even distribution with nothing remarkable happening. What would be great though is if we could see how often a win occurred in each situation. Now that would be interesting to see, but what does it mean to win, and how does myNumber help us to figure that out?

Let's start by tracking these wins. Just inside the for-loop, right at the top, add another variable called win and set it to false.

```
var win = false
```

The next step is to reveal one of the two numbers and compare it to our own generated myNumber. There's some new logic we need to apply here. We need to decide *how* we're going to be using myNumber. This is going to involve making some assumptions.

Ultimately, we're trying to work out which number out of firstNumber or secondNumber is the largest. To make this simple, we'll have the simulation always choose firstNumber for the reveal. So, we'll compare myNumber to firstNumber, and depending on which one is larger, we take a guess at what secondNumber might be using the same rules every time. For example:

1. If myNumber is smaller than firstNumber, then let us assume firstNumber is larger than secondNumber.

2. If myNumber is larger than firstNumber, then let us assume firstNumber is smaller than secondNumber.

If either of these assumptions turns out to be correct, this will set the win property to true (we'll use this a bit later).

Inside the for-loop, after all properties, let's make some comparisons.

```
if myNumber < firstNumber && firstNumber > secondNumber {
    win = true
    numberOfCorrectGuesses += 1
```

```
} else if myNumber > firstNumber && firstNumber < secondNumber {
    win = true
    numberOfCorrectGuesses += 1
}
```

Before you run the playground, make sure that you have your logging statement at the bottom of the file.

```
print("correctly guessed \(numberOfCorrectGuesses) times out of \
(numberOfPuzzles)")
```

Run the playground a few times and you'll notice something a little strange. The number of correct guesses should now be sitting at around the 600–700 range, but earlier we were getting results between 450 and 550. What gives?

It looks like we *can* do better than 50/50; but how?

Magic or Logic?

We're no longer guessing which number is larger from the toss of a coin, but instead on some well-thought-out logical rules. We need to apply some more logging here to drill down further into why a comparison to another unrelated random number actually works.

As we saw, there are only three possible outcomes for the myNumber properties position in relation to the other two numbers.

1. myNumber is smaller than firstNumber and secondNumber.

2. myNymber is larger than firstNumber and secondNumber.

3. myNumber is between firstNumber and secondNumber.

Earlier on we saw that myNumber would always fall equally between these categories. This time however, now that we can keep track of wins, we're going to see if the distribution of wins falls within the same equal pattern. My guess is that this isn't the case; otherwise we wouldn't be seeing any improvement in our guesses.

At the bottom of the for-loop, add the following code:

```
guard win == true else { continue }

if myNumber >= max(firstNumber, secondNumber) {
    timesMyNumberIsLargest += 1
} else if myNumber <= min(firstNumber, secondNumber) {
    timesMyNumberIsSmallest += 1
} else {
    timesMyNumberIsInBetween += 1
}
```

On the first line here, I've introduced something called a guard. It's like the opposite to an if statement. In this case, win must hold a value of true; otherwise the code following the guard will not execute. If it's false, the code in the curly braces is run instead. Here we've put a continue. This informs the for-loop to skip the rest of the code in the current iteration and *continue* to the next one. If instead we were to use a return, the loop would exit completely.

We have this in place because we're only tracking win states now.

The code following this is the same we had earlier, but this time the properties are only being incremented when there's a win!

Slightly adjust our print statements and then run the playground again to see what we got.

```
print("largest guess won \(timesMyNumberIsLargest) times.")
print("smallest guess won \(timesMyNumberIsSmallest) times.")
print("inbetween guess won \(timesMyNumberIsInBetween) times.")
```

Let's run the playground again and see what we get.

```
largest guess won 171 times.
smallest guess won 177 times.
inbetween guess won 338 times.
correctly guessed 686 times out of 1000
```

Now that's an unequal distribution!

It looks like we have our answer. Doing a little math here, we can see that when myNumber falls into either the largest or smallest categories, it looks like the chance of winning is still around 50%. But, when myNumber is *between* both numbers, it's a guaranteed win! That's what gives us the edge. Only a slight edge, but it's enough to be significant over a number of games. If you were to challenge a friend to many rounds of this game, used this strategy, and put money on it, you're certain to come out richer than you started.

Cheating the Guessing Game

Winning 66% of the time is great and all, but what if we can make it so we can win 90% of the time? By setting a lower and upper bound for the numbers your friend can choose from, we should be able to take more control of the outcome.

We can place this limit on firstNumber and secondNumber with the following code:

```
let firstNumber = Int.random(in: 490_000..<510_000)
let secondNumber = Int.random(in: 490_000..<510_000)
```

firstNumber and secondNumber are now random integers between 490,000 and 510,000. That's a range of 20,000 different numbers, while still keeping myNumber between 0 and 1,000,000.

Run the playground again and you'll find that the chances of winning are remarkably reduced. The odds are now back down to around 50%. With myNumber having such a large range and your friends' numbers being limited to a narrow portion of that range, myNumber will almost never fall between your friends' numbers, thus eliminating a guaranteed win.

We prefer to win more often; otherwise there's no point to cheating. Let's make a slight change here. If you were to give your friend a range of numbers with a large enough gap between them, you *should* win almost every time!

Make the following edits to firstNumber and secondNumber:

```
let firstNumber = Int.random(in: 0..<20)
let secondNumber = Int.random(in: 999_980..<1_000_000)
```

1. firstNumber must be between 0 and 20.

2. secondNumber must be between 999,980 and 1,000,000.

This change limits firstNumber and secondNumber to the lower and upper ends of the millions of numbers that myNumber has access to. If you run the playground again, you'll see that myNumber falls between firstNumber and secondNumber almost every game. Unfortunately, this little scheme would be very apparent to your friend. It would actually be far easier and less obvious if *they* were to "cheat" (not really, because there are no rules against it) by just choosing two numbers that are very close. In fact, if they chose two numbers that were directly next to each other, generating your own number wouldn't really give you any benefit at all, and we'd be back to where we started.

Results

Is there a way for you to get a better than 50/50 odds when playing the Guessing Game?

It's counterintuitive, but the answer is definitely yes. Introducing another random number that is entirely unrelated to the first two chosen numbers *will* increase your chances of winning the game. This works because when we add a new number to the game, we're also increasing the number of possible outcomes available to us. Rather than having a simple choice of "larger" or "smaller" (50/50), we've given ourselves a third option, "between."

Just to be sure, I ran the simulation a few more times and tracked the results (Figure 3-1).

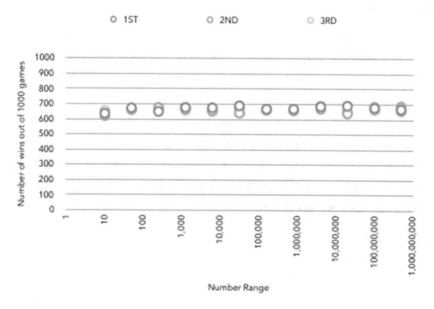

Figure 3-1. *Result distribution across 1000 games using a number range of 0 to 1,000,000,000*

myNumber, firstNumber, and secondNumber are generated from the number ranges in the first column. Multiplying by five after each run-through of a thousand games. This process was repeated two more times for 3,000 games at each number range. I ran these for a total of 36,000 games. From number ranges of 10 to nearly 500 million (not shown in table).

There was some hope that as the range of numbers increased, so too did the likelihood of myNumber falling between firstNumber and secondNumber. From these results, this is not the case. Providing that both players in the guessing game are using the same range, the person guessing has around 66% chance of guessing correctly.

Summary

These first few projects have been all about getting to know Swift and working within the playground environment. In this chapter we've expanded even more on this by introducing some extra built-in tools such as the min/max functions and guard statements.

We also further solidified what we learned about trusting our intuition when it comes to making predictions around probability.

So far we've made great progress, and in the next chapter, we'll ramp things up even more, and I'll introduce you to a few little tools that will prepare you for even greater challenges ahead!

CHAPTER 4

Theatre Seating

This time around I'll be introducing some new data types and walk you through how you can create your own. While they're not completely necessary to complete the tasks in this chapter, they will make things a little easier to understand what's going on and become essential tools for us to use in future projects.

Further on in the chapter, we'll make use of separate source files. You have noticed that your playgrounds spend a lot of time logging their output. Sometimes you'll even see the numbers in the side bar continue to clime, long after you get an output in the debug area. Playgrounds are slow, and they in no way reflect the performance of this code running in the real world. Looping over a million items in an array in a playground can take about 30 seconds to complete (depending on hardware), whereas in a real program, we could see almost instant results. This slowdown comes from all that logging, so we need to move the bulk of our computational code into a separate background file. The projects ahead will require some extra computing power to execute in a reasonable amount of time (minutes vs. seconds), and there's no point wasting the power that we do have on logging.

So first up we'll have a short overview of classes, structs, and functions. Then I'll show you how to split your code into multiple files, which will help to speed up your playground code.

© Beau Nouvelle 2019
B. Nouvelle, *Simulations in Swift 5*, https://doi.org/10.1007/978-1-4842-5337-3_4

Structs, Classes, and Functions

It's not my intention to write a "Learn Swift" or "How to Code" book. There are plenty of those available already, so this next part is merely a brief overview. If you're already familiar with these concepts, go right ahead and skip this section. If, however, you're after a more in-depth explanation than what I'm offering, you can download Apple's own reference books on Swift for free from the iBook store.

What Are Structs?

Structs are value type objects. Any time an assignment is made, the object is copied. This gives you two distinct objects. These are great for storing and passing around data that you don't plan on changing often. They can be initialized quickly with very little overhead.

```
// Both variables have a value of 1, but they are two distinct
and separate objects.
var a = 1
var b = a

print(a) // 1
print(b) // 1

// If we modify a, b remains unchanged even though it was
created from a.
a = 2
print(a) // 2
print(b) // 1
```

This makes a lot of sense because it's similar to how we would expect things to behave in the real world. Structs are mainly used for storing data; for example, you might have a Person struct to store someone's height, age, and gender. You'll then be able to pass this object around your program without having to worry about some other code making changes to it. Any time a change is made, a copy is created, leaving the original as it was.

What Are Classes?

Classes are reference type objects. This means that you're passing around a reference to a value and not the value itself.

These references are called *pointers* and they took me a while to get my head around when I was new to programming. Pointers point to a value; they don't *hold* that value themselves. You can have many pointers pointing to a single value. This is great for when you need to alter an object in one place within your code and have access to those changes elsewhere simultaneously.

```
var a = someClass()
var b = a
print(a) // someClass
print(b) // someClass

// Changing the value of a, changes the value of b.
a = otherClass()
print(a) // otherClass
print(b) // otherClass
```

What Are Functions?

Functions allow us to wrap our code up to make it more reusable. In most applications, we'll want to run the same operations many times, and rather than writing it each time we want to use it, we can just call a function instead.

```
func doMath(number: Int) {
    let square = number * number
    let result = square + 5
    print(result)
}

doMath(number: 2) // 9
doMath(number: 3) // 14
doMath(number: 4) // 21
```

Furthermore, classes and structs are wrappers around our functions. They allow us to pass around related groups of functions to different parts of our code.

I told you it would be brief, and it's nowhere near complete, but we'll be working with classes, structs, and functions throughout the rest of this book. It's important that you have some understanding of what these are.

Theatre Seating Problem

Doors have just opened and people are pouring into the theatre. Everyone is assigned to one of the 100 seats available. However, the first person in line has misplaced their ticket and has instead decided to sit down in a random chair. The second person will either sit in their assigned seat if it's available; otherwise they will choose from a random one among those remaining. Each person following obeys the same rules as the second person.

What is the probability that the 100th person will be able to sit in their assigned seat?

Planning

Let's break the problem down into a few simple steps.

1. Generate 100 seats with 100 people to fill them.

2. The first person chooses a random seat.

3. Next person sits in their assigned seat if it's still available. If it's not, then they will pick a random seat.

4. Repeat steps 2 and 3 to fill all chairs.

5. If the last seat filled is the last seat available, then we keep track of when this happens.

6. Repeat steps 1–5 a hundred times so that we can collect a large enough sample size.

New Playground

Create a new playground and name it TheatreSeating. The next thing we need to take care of is generating a theatre full of seats, and a large group of people to fill those seats.

Your First Struct

We'll begin by adding the following code to the playground:

```
struct Person {
    let assignedSeat: Int
}
```

```
struct Seat {
    let number: Int
    var person: Person?
}
```

Here we're using two structs to create two new types: Person and Seat. Person has a property called assignedSeat—this will be the seat number the person *should* be sitting in.

Seat has two properties, number and person. When someone is sitting in the seat, person will have a Person assigned to it, but until then it will remain empty.

With structs we can create our own value types. Just like how Int is a value type, so are Person and Seat.

Your First Class

In this chapter, we'll also be creating our first class, and this will be the model for the theatre in our simulation.

Write this code below the two structs we just added.

```
class Theatre {
}
```

This class will hold the bulk of the code we'll be using for this simulation. Let's add some properties.

```
class Theatre {
    let capacity: Int
    private var seats = [Seat]()
    private var people = [Person]()
}
```

Our Theatre class has a capacity property that will allow us to set the number of seats available while also doubling as the number of people to fill them.

We've also created two arrays. These are marked with the private keyword because we don't want to allow them to be modified externally. This means that any code outside the enclosing curly braces for this class cannot interact with these properties in any way.

There's now an error in the playground indicating that Theatre has no initializers. You can clean up this error by creating an initializer function or setting the classes properties to some initial value directly.

The seats and people properties have already been initialized with empty arrays; capacity on the other hand has a let keyword, but more importantly, no assignment. The compiler is complaining about this, and it's why we have an error. We're going to solve this by creating an initializer function for our Theatre class and assigning a value to capacity there. This way, when we want to make use of this class in our program, we'll be forced to pass in a value for capacity at that time. Setting the capacity at initialization means we can use a different value each time we create a theatre. Just below the three properties, but before the closing curly brace, we'll add our first function.

```
init(capacity: Int) {
    self.capacity = capacity
}
```

This function will hold all of our setup code to get a theatre up and running. So far it accepts a parameter of the type **Int** and assigns it to the capacity property we created earlier. After adding this code, the error should now disappear.

This is what's called a designated initializer. This is required to be called when initializing a new Theatre class. Designated initializers set up all properties defined in that class. This ensures that we don't forget to assign a value to the capacity property.

As it stands, both seats and people are empty. It's no good to have a theatre with nowhere to sit. Now that we have a value coming through for the theatre's capacity, we can start adding items to these two arrays.

First of all, we need to initialize each seat with a number. As with capacity on our Theatre class, the number property has the let keyword and no default value. Unlike classes though, structures give us a designated initializer for free, so we can just call that to create a seat! We'll use this to fill out both Person *and* Seat arrays.

Inside our Theatre classes init function, add this for-loop and its contents below the capacity assignment.

```
for seatNumber in 0..<capacity {
    let seat = Seat(number: seatNumber, person: nil)
    seats.append(seat)
}
```

The index of the loop will be the seatNumber. Starting from 0 all the way up to whatever value we have assigned to capacity.

On each loop through we create a Seat and add it to the seats array. Let's go ahead and create our line of people by adding similar code before the closing brace of the for-loop.

```
let person = Person(assignedSeat: seatNumber)
people.append(person)
```

We now have a line of people waiting to get in and enough seats to fit them all. What an excellent line it is too, with everyone in perfect order. It's such a shame that the first person through will be messing it all up.

Outside the for-loop but still inside the init function, we'll get the first person in line to choose a random seat.

```
let randomSeatNumber = Int.random(in: 0..<capacity)
seats[randomSeatNumber].person = people.removeFirst()
```

Here we're using `Int.random` to generate ourselves an integer between 0 and `capacity`. This number is used to pick a random seat from the `seats` array and put a person in it from the `people` array. We do this by calling `removeFirst()` on the `people` array. This function removes the first item in the array and returns it—if it exists. We must remove this person from the line. Later on, we'll be looping over this array and filling the seats one by one. We can't put this person in two different chairs. In fact, besides removing the first person, the line will remain unaffected throughout this project, and the people in it will stay standing. Due to how structs copy their values, it will be the clones of those waiting in line that will be filling the chairs in the theatre. Simulation life is a cruel one.

Seating a Person

At this point we can start working on the code that will put people in their seats. We'll create a new function inside the Theatre class and have that handle putting someone into a seat.

```
func sit(person: Person, in seatNumber: Int) {

}
```

The first thing we have to ensure when putting someone into a chair is to check that the chair is currently vacant. So inside the newly created function, add this code:

```
if seats[seatNumber].person == nil {
    seats[seatNumber].person = person
}
```

This first checks that the `person` property on a seat at the `seatNumber` position in the array is `nil`; if it is, we'll put the person passed into the function there.

Now that this has been taken care of, we still need to write something that can handle the event where someone is already occupying the seat. What we'll do is generate a random seat number and check if a person is already sitting there, and if someone is already sitting there, we'll generate *another* random seat number, and then we'll check if someone is already sitting there and—wait a second. It seems like we'll be here writing our code forever!

What we can do though is employ a little technique where we'll make this function call itself over and over again until it can find an empty spot for a person to sit!

The sit() function already has a person and seatNumber parameter. If the seat is not vacant, we can just call it again and change seatNumber to something random.

```
else {
    let randomSeat = Int.random(in: 0..<seats.count)
    sit(person: person, in: randomSeat)
}
```

The entire function body should now look something like this:

```
func sit(person: Person, in seatNumber: Int) {
    if seats[seatNumber].person == nil {
        seats[seatNumber].person = person
    } else {
        let randomSeat = Int.random(in: 0..<seats.count)
        sit(person: person, in: randomSeat)
    }
}
```

It's not the most efficient piece of code, but we should never really approach a new problem we want to solve with these concerns slowing us down. The priority is getting it working. Brute-forcing a solution is better than no solution. You can always make refinements later. In this case, the inefficiencies reside in how we're generating the random seat number when a spot is filled. It's possible the next random seat is also taken, and the one after that; in fact, the more the theatre is filled, the more often a taken seat number will be generated. This can waste precious processing time. We'll leave it for now though, and if it becomes a problem, we can always come back to this function and have a look at improving our algorithm.

Seating Many People

Great, but we're not seating just one person, we're seating a hundred of them... or more! Rather than call sit() manually a hundred times, we should put this in a loop.

We'll create a new function and call it sitPeople.

```
func sitPeople() {
}
```

Inside we'll write some code that will loop over the number of people waiting to be seated. Both the number of seats and people are the same, so this works fine. In the future you might decide to set the quantity of them separately, so in that case you would loop over whichever group has fewer items.

```
for person in people {
    sit(person: person, in: person.assignedSeat)
}
```

We pull a person out of the people array and tell them to sit in their assigned seat.

Running the Simulation

Right now nothing will be happening because we haven't called any functions outside of our classes or structs. They're there, ready to be used, but nothing is using them. So let's do that now.

At the bottom of the playground, outside the Theatre class, add these two lines of code:

```
let theatre = Theatre(capacity: 100)
theatre.sitPeople()
```

Here we create a new theatre with a seating capacity of 100, then we tell it to sit everyone. Your code should now be running fine with no errors. In the side bar to the right, you'll see some output but nothing useful.

Now we're up to step 5. If you don't remember, that was to do with keeping track of when—or if—the last person sits in their assigned seat.

An easy way to do this would be to check the last seat in the theatre and compare its number to the assigned seat number of the person sitting in it.

At the moment we can't access seats from outside the class because we marked it as private. What we can do though is make it read-only. This allows outside code to *view* the seats property but not make any changes to it. To do this, add the (set) keyword after private.

```
private(set) var seats = [Seat]()
```

The value can now be set and read privately, but only read publicly.

Jumping back outside the class and the bottom of the playground, let's compare seat numbers.

```
let lastSeat = theatre.seats.last

if lastSeat?.person?.assignedSeat == lastSeat?.number {
    print("Last person is in correct seat")
```

```
} else {
    print("Last person is in wrong seat")
}
```

Since we've been giving our variables descriptive names, the preceding code should be easy enough to follow. This is just one run-through of the simulation. That's nowhere near enough data. We'll need to run it a few more times to get any answers.

A Hundred Theatres

It's time to run our simulation a hundred times. We could do this manually and keep track of how many times the last seat and that person's number matches up, but we're programmers, and would automate everything if we could.

```
var lastPersonInAssignedSeat = 0
for _ in 0..<100 {
    let theatre = Theatre(capacity: 100)
    theatre.sitPeople()

    let lastSeat = theatre.seats.last

    if lastSeat?.person?.assignedSeat == lastSeat?.number {
        lastPersonInAssignedSeat += 1
    }
}

print(lastPersonInAssignedSeat)
```

Here we've created a for-loop and wrapped that around the code we wrote in the previous section. The loop will run through a hundred times, generating a hundred theatres and seating a hundred people in each. We've also added a new variable so that we can track the number of times the last person makes it to their assigned seat.

Run the playground.

You might notice that this is taking significantly longer to execute. If you were patient enough to wait for the results, you'd see something surprising. If not, incoming spoilers.

About 50% of the time the last person seated will be in the correct place. Since we can't double-check this figure in a reasonable amount of time, let's make some speed improvements.

Supercharging the Playground

As briefly mentioned at the start of this chapter, the most significant cause of slow playgrounds is the amount of logging going on. A way to avoid this overhead is to move your code into separate files, thereby cutting them off from that side bar.

We already have our class and structs organized quite well, so it should be easy enough to split those all up into separate files.

To get started, open up the left panel of your playground, right-click the *Sources* folder, and select *New File*, as shown in Figure 4-1. **Remember, the left panel can be opened by clicking on the button with the left vertical line at the top right of the playground window**.

Figure 4-1. Pop-up window showing how to add a new file to the playground sources folder

Rename this file to Person.swift and cut/paste the Person struct from your TheatreSeating playground into this file.

Repeat the same steps for both Seat.swift and Theatre.swift.

You should only have a few lines of code remaining in the main playground file.

Make It Public

We have another error. The playground can no longer find the Theatre class. We'll need to expose the code inside the newly created files before the playground can pick them up.

Let's start with our Person struct. So open up Person.swift. Mark both the struct and assignedSeat property with the public keyword.

```
public struct Person {
    public let assignedSeat: Int
}
```

Now we'll do the same for `Seat.swift`.

```
public struct Seat {
    public let number: Int
    public var person: Person?
}
```

Inside `Theatre.swift` we have a few extra areas to make public. First mark the entire class as public by adding the `public` keyword before `class`.

```
public class Theatre {...}
```

Next we'll mark the `seats` as `public`, but we'll still keep the `private(set)` keywords we added earlier. We're opening up this property to be read-only throughout the rest of the playground but still restricting its value to being set internally (can only be set by code inside the Theatre class).

```
public private(set) var seats = [Seat]()
```

The `init(capacity:)` and `sitPeople()` function will also need to be made public.

```
public init(capacity: Int) {...}
public func sitPeople() {...}
```

That should be all we need to do. Go back to the main playground file and run it one last time.

From Minutes to Seconds

Instead of taking a few minutes to execute, you should now be getting results from the simulation almost immediately.

We'll be making use of extra source files a lot more as we progress through this book. The simulations will continue to grow in complexity and will require the extra computing power. We need them to run fast!

Summary

I threw a lot of new stuff at you in this chapter—classes, structs, functions—and even some more advanced programming techniques like recursion.

You also learned about the performance difficulties we can run into when executing heavy compute tasks within playgrounds and discovered how to mitigate these issues by moving code out of the main project file.

We're now done with building simulations to find answers to specific puzzles or problems that need to be solved. Instead, we'll now be focusing on more open-ended designs. The real fun stuff. I think you're ready for it.

CHAPTER 5

Projectile Motion

Up until now we've been able to avoid some of the more math-heavy simulations. While projectile motion *can* include some very intense calculations, I promise to keep things simple throughout this chapter (the *really* tricky stuff is coming later).

Projectile motion is the kind of motion experienced by objects that are thrown, ejected, or launched. If we know an object's initial speed, angle, and direction of movement, we can perform some calculations to predict where it will end up.

Thinking About Gravity

Gravity affects everything around us. This applies to the entire universe. Newton's first law of motion states that a body will remain at rest unless an outside force acts on it and a body in motion will remain in motion in a straight line until an external force interacts with it. For our simulation, this external force is gravity.

Objects on Earth accelerate toward the ground at around $9.8 m/s^2$—this is an average; it differs depending on where you are on the Earth's surface. This means that for every second an object is falling, its speed is increasing by 9.8m/s. At 10 seconds, an object will be falling at almost 100 meters per second and would have covered a total distance of roughly 500 meters. See Figure 5-1.

© Beau Nouvelle 2019
B. Nouvelle, *Simulations in Swift 5*, https://doi.org/10.1007/978-1-4842-5337-3_5

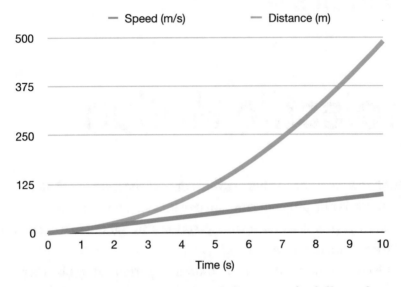

Figure 5-1. *Comparison of speed and distance of a falling object over time*

The formula for calculating the speed of a falling object on Earth, from rest, in a vacuum, is `seconds * 9.8`. Air resistance can have a significant effect on how fast a falling object picks up speed and the maximum velocity it can reach. To keep things simple for our experiments, we're just going to ignore air resistance altogether. All objects fall at the same rate in a vacuum, so we'll assume this is where our simulation takes place.

New Playground

Let's create a new playground and name it `ProjectileMotion`. We'll need to build up our simulation one step at a time and test it as we go. This way we can be sure our math is correct before moving to the next step.

The first thing we'll begin with is simulating a falling object from rest. We can compare the above charts with our results to ensure that we're on the right track.

Creating Gravity

Start by adding two new properties to the playground, gravity and
deltaTime. We'll mark these with the let keyword to indicate that we
don't want to allow anything to change them during the execution of the
playground. Gravity is a constant after all. Or is it?

```
let gravity: Double = -9.8
```

Gravity is set to a *negative* value to indicate movement in a downward
direction. Alternatively, any object in the simulation moving in an upward
direction will have a positive y velocity.

Currently the object will begin at the height of zero and start falling at a
rate of $9.8m/s^2$.

I highly encourage you to play around with a few other values once
you've completed this chapter, so I've included a list of notable objects in
our solar system in Table 5-1.

Table 5-1. *Notable solar system objects with their gravitational acceleration*

Name	Gravity m/s
Sun	273.95
Jupiter	24.79
Neptune	11.15
Saturn	10.44
Earth	9.8
Venus	8.87
Uranus	8.69
Mars	3.71
Mercury	3.7
Moon	1.62
Pluto	0.62

Delta Time

Delta time—most commonly written as dt—is a concept we use in programming for measuring the elapsed time between events. In graphics programming, this is usually the time passed since the last frame update.

```
let deltaTime: Double = 1
```

Without deltaTime, if a game running at 60fps wants to move a character forward at 60m/s, it would have to move the character 1 meter each frame. However, if the frame rate should drop to 30fps, the character, still moving at 1 meter each frame, would only end up moving 30 meters in the same amount of time. If a game's frame rate jumps all over the place, the character won't move smoothly across the screen at all!

With deltaTime the character's movement is calculated based on the time *between* each frame. At 60fps the character will move 1 meter per frame, and at 30fps the character will move 2 meters for each frame. In this scenario, the frame rate is less of an issue. The character will move the same distance each second if the game is running at 60fps or 30fps.

In our simulation, deltaTime won't be based on frame rates. Instead, we'll be using it to modify the number of calculations performed per second. The math we'll be using to calculate a trajectory can only give us an estimate, and the more times we can perform a calculation per second, the more accurate our results will be.

Velocity, Displacement, and Time

We'll need to keep track of our object's velocity over time. So, let's create a variable for that. While we're at it, we'll also need to monitor the vertical distance traveled and the amount of time elapsed.

```
var velocity: Double = 0
var verticalDisplacement: Double = 0
var secondsElapsed: Double = 0
```

While-Loops

Up until now most of the simulations we've built have employed a for-loop in one way or another. This chapter introduces you to the while-loop. For-loops are usually used in cases where you have a predetermined number of iterations—like the number of items in an array. While-loops on the other hand will continue until some condition is met. We use these in cases where we don't know how many times we need to loop through something.

To give you an example, take a look at these two blocks of code. The first one will only run the print statement five times before exiting. The second block of code will run until a random number generator produces the number 20. It could take just one iteration to produce 20, or it could take a thousand.

```
for index in 0..<5 {
    print(index)
}

var randomNumber = 0
while randomNumber != 20 {
    randomNumber = Int.random(in: 0..<100)
}
```

We'll be basing our while-loop on the secondsElapsed property which will allow us to set a limit to how long the simulation should run. We'll also get the benefit of being able to split the seconds into smaller chunks, giving us much more control each loop.

```
while secondsElapsed <= 10 {
    secondsElapsed += deltaTime
}
```

Now, unlike a for-loop where you can specify a set number of iterations, the while–loop will run forever if it doesn't meet its condition. This means you *must* have a way for the loop to exit. If it runs forever, your playground will eventually slow down and freeze. When this happens, you'll likely need to restart Xcode. Outside of playgrounds, it's not so bad, but because we have auto-run turned on, while-loops can be a problem. So, it is always good to have a safeguard in place right away, but for us, incrementing secondsElapsed until it reaches the exit number of 10 should be fine.

The while-loop will run ten times, but not much else is happening so let's put some calculations in there.

Calculating Velocity

As mentioned earlier, we can calculate an object's velocity by using
`seconds * gravity`, but since we're running a simulation and making
use of delta time, we'll do the calculation a little differently. Add the
following code inside the while-loop, above the code that increments
`secondsElapsed`:

```
velocity += gravity * deltaTime
print("vel: \(velocity), dis: \(verticalDisplacement)")
```

We have our current velocity, which at the start of the simulation
is zero. Since `deltaTime` is set to one second, the product of `gravity`
and `deltaTime` is always -9.8. Each loop through decreases the velocity
value by 9.8.

Calculating Distance

The next thing we might want to do is work out how far the object falls
every second. This value will change as time goes on, and as the object's
speed increases, the distance covered each second does too.

Add this line of code just before the print statement inside the while-loop.

```
verticalDisplacement += velocity * deltaTime
```

At this point let's compare our outputs to ensure we're on the right path.
vel: -9.8, dis: -9.8
vel: -19.6, dis: -29.400000000000002
vel: -29.400000000000002, dis: -58.800000000000004
vel: -39.2, dis: -98.0
vel: -49.0, dis: -147.0
vel: -58.8, dis: -205.8
vel: -68.6, dis: -274.4

vel: -78.39999999999999, dis: -352.79999999999995

vel: -88.19999999999999, dis: -440.99999999999994

vel: -97.99999999999999, dis: -538.9999999999999

vel: -107.79999999999998, dis: -646.7999999999998

If your results look anything like this, then you're good to move to the next section.

Graphing

Playgrounds have a neat feature that let you visualize what your code is doing. If you click the small little squares inside the side bar on the right, you'll get a nice little line graph embedded in your code for both `velocity` and `verticalDisplacement`. Notice in Figure 5-2 that they have different rates of change.

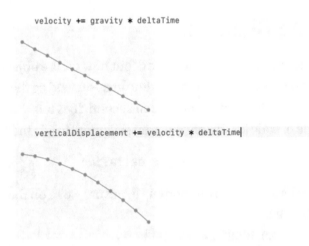

Figure 5-2. *A comparison of verticalDisplacement and velocity*

With `velocity` and `verticalDisplacement` set to zero, the object will merely fall and increase its speed linearly. It's not all that interesting. So, let's play around with the numbers for a bit.

Set the velocity to 50 and you'll see the vertical displacement graph show the projectile going up before slowing, then falling back down. See Figure 5-3.

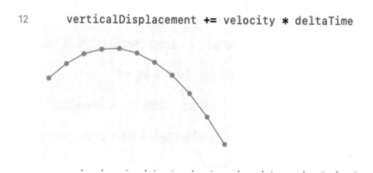

```
12      verticalDisplacement += velocity * deltaTime
```

Figure 5-3. *Changes in verticalDisplacement graphed at each iteration through the while-loop*

This feature will chart just about any number you put in there. As a fun little side note, here are some other graphable functions you might like to try out within the while-loop.

```
cos(verticalDisplacement)
sin(velocity)
Int.random(in: 0..<10)
tan(velocity)
```

Make sure that you remember to remove these changes before moving on to the next section.

Improving Accuracy

I think by now you may have realized that the results are a little off. Changes in velocity in the real world are gradual, but in our simulation, they occur in steps. -9.8m/s is only applied to the velocity once each second. This is inaccurate because the object wasn't falling at that velocity for the entire second. After half a second, the effect of gravity would have only been -4.9m/s.

Over time our results will divert far from the correct results. However, there are two ways we can solve this. We can perform our calculations multiple times per second to reduce error rate, or use an actual free-fall equation.

$$d = v_0 * t + 0.5 * g * t^2$$

If we plug in our variables, it looks a little more like this:

$$displacement = velocity * seconds + 0.5 * gravity * seconds^2$$

Then with numbers and a result:

$$d = 50 * 10 + 0.5 * -9.8 * 10^2 = 10$$

The object will be sitting at 10 meters *above* the starting point after 10 seconds. How? Because the initial velocity of 50 is shooting the object up, and 10 seconds just isn't enough time to have that object fall back to its original starting position.

Compare this to the final `verticalDisplacement` of our simulation, which ends up at around -96 meters. Have we made a mistake?

Not quite. We're creating a simulation here, and sometimes you don't have access to nice clean formulas. The best you can do is try to get as close to the correct results as possible. The -96 value is just an approximate, and it's one we can certainly improve on.

We just need to run through the calculations much more frequently. The less time that passes between them, the more accurate our results.

For this exercise we'll use the formula as a safety net, to ensure that our simulation is working correctly.

Change the value of `deltaTime` to `0.5` and you'll see that the loop runs twice as many times as before. The debug area has also output twice as much data, and the simulation takes twice as long to finish. However, total time passed within the simulator is still limited to 10 seconds.

For now, let's forget about where the object will be at the end of the simulation and focus on figuring out its maximum vertical displacement instead. This will give you a better idea of how reducing `deltaTime` can give us more accurate results.

Here's a little snippet from the middle of my results after having set `deltaTime` to 0.5:

...

vel: 10.800000000000008, dis: 111.80000000000003
vel: 5.9000000000000075, dis: 114.75000000000003
vel: 1.000000000000007, dis: 115.25000000000003
vel: -3.8999999999999932, dis: 113.30000000000003
vel: -8.799999999999994, dis: 108.90000000000003
vel: -13.699999999999994, dis: 102.05000000000004

...

The maximum height reached is where the velocity is reduced to zero. This is the peak, right before the object starts falling. With a `deltaTime` of 0.5, we can see a peak displacement of 115.25 meters. That is, the object reaches a maximum height of 115.25 meters before falling back down again.

The gap in velocity calculations is still quite large though. It goes from 1.0 to -3.9. I suspect there's more room in there for a larger vertical displacement.

Try setting `deltaTime` to 0.05.

vel: 0.509999999999974, dis: 126.30049999999981
vel: 0.019999999999973983, dis: 126.30149999999982
vel: -0.47000000000002606, dis: 126.27799999999982
vel: -0.9600000000000262, dis: 126.22999999999982

Now the maximum calculated height is 126.30. The real value is around 127.5, but getting there requires us to reduce the value of `deltaTime` even further.

The more calculations we perform, the more accurate the results; but soon performance becomes an issue. This is similar to playing a video game at maximum graphical settings on a computer that isn't quite powerful enough. Sure, it may render all the details, but it might only be able to do that at two frames per second. To keep our simulation running fast, we'll need to sacrifice a little accuracy for performance.

Calculating Angles

So far our simulation can only simulate projectiles moving vertically, but we want to be able to shoot them over vast distances. Don't worry if high school mathematics was a long time ago. I won't be going into it here. If you want to find out more, Khan Academy has some excellent free videos on projectile motion.

Before we start, remove the print statement inside the while-loop. We'll be adding some better logging a little bit later, and we want to ensure the playground is running as fast as possible while we build out our simulation.

At the top of our playground, underneath where we have created the deltaTime property, add a new one called angle.

```
let angle: Double = 45 * (.pi / 180)
```

We're setting it to 45 degrees to start with as that will give us a nice even split between vertical and horizontal velocities.

The little bit of math we're doing at the end of that line is there to convert the degrees into radians.

We also need to move velocity up into the same section (with the other lets) and change it to a let. Our simulation won't be changing its value this time.

```
let velocity: Double = 50
```

Next, we'll add a few more properties to the bottom of the var list.

```
var horizontalVelocity = velocity * cos(angle)
var horizontalDisplacement: Double = 0
var verticalVelocity = velocity * sin(angle)
```

When you're done the complete list of properties should look like this:

```
let gravity: Double = -9.8
let deltaTime: Double = 0.05

let angle: Double = 45 * (.pi / 180)
let velocity: Double = 50

var verticalDisplacement: Double = 0
var secondsElapsed: Double = 0
var horizontalVelocity = velocity * cos(angle)
var horizontalDisplacement: Double = 0
var verticalVelocity = velocity * sin(angle)
```

Xcode will now show a compile error, but we'll get to fixing that soon.

Most of us should vaguely remember sine and cosine from high school trigonometry. We're converting angles to radians, so for our calculations, an angle of 45 degrees becomes 0.785 radians; plugging that into cos() and sin(), we get around 0.707 for both. If we then multiply that by the object's starting velocity, cos (horizontal) and sin (vertical) will return both horizontal and vertical velocities. Because it's 45 degrees, these velocities will be the same and will continue to be the same until another force acts on them.

Delete everything inside the while-loop except for secondsElapsed += deltaTime. We'll keep this at the top and write the rest of the code below it. Remember, if you don't have anything to satisfy the loops condition, it will continue forever and freeze your playground!

The first line we are going to write in there will calculate the vertical displacement—the height of our object at any moment in the simulation.

```
verticalDisplacement += verticalVelocity * deltaTime
```

Then we re-calculate the vertical velocity of the object due to gravity's influence.

```
verticalVelocity += gravity * deltaTime
```

Now we get to work out the horizontal displacement. The thing about horizontal velocity is that it never changes. It's not under the influence of gravity, so it will continue until another force comes in to play. This other force could be the ground, a wall, or another object.

```
horizontalDisplacement += horizontalVelocity * deltaTime
```

That's all we need to do. The math is complete. But we still need to make some more improvements.

Let's add a new property to the top of our playground, under `velocity`, and call it `height`. This will be the object's initial vertical displacement.

```
let height: Double = 0
```

Then, change `verticalDisplacement`'s initial value from 0 to `height`. This makes things a little cleaner by keeping all our user-applied settings in one place and our variables in another.

Another thing we might want to do is end the simulation early once our projectile has hit the ground. Write the following inside the while-loop, just after the opening brace:

```
if verticalDisplacement < 0 {
    break
}
```

In this this case, if the verticalDisplacement drops below zero, the loop will *break* out and exit early. We could have made verticalDisplacement the condition for the while-loop, but I think having some extra control over the length of time the simulation should run for is more important and explicit.

Logging

There are a few things that we're interested in as an output.

1. Maximum horizontal distance traveled.

2. Maximum vertical distance traveled.

3. How much time has passed before the projectile hits the ground?

To get started on the first one, we can just add a print statement using horizontalDisplacement at the bottom of the playground file, outside the while-loop.

```
print("Max Length:", horizontalDisplacement)
```

If you run it now, you should get an output that reads Max Length: 282.8. Providing the starting conditions are with a velocity of 50 and angle set to 45, and deltaTime is 0.5.

For the second output, we'll need to add a new variable. Add maxHeight at the top of the file, below verticalVelocity.

```
var maxHeight: Double = 0
```

At the end of the while-loop, we need to wrap our `maxHeight` assignment in an if statement since we're only interested in the condition where the projectile is moving up, not coming down.

```
if verticalDisplacement > maxHeight {
    maxHeight = verticalDisplacement
}
```

Add another print statement at the bottom of the playground, outside the while-loop.

```
print("Max Height:", maxHeight)
```

Max Height: 72.82135

All we have to do for the third output is print `secondsElapsed`.

```
print("Seconds Elapsed:", secondsElapsed)
```

Max Length 282.842712474619
Max Height: 72.82135623730949
Seconds Elapsed: 8.0

You should have similar outputs, at least to a few decimal places.

Remember, these results aren't entirely accurate. So, don't go building rockets or trebuchets (obviously the superior siege engine) with this little living calculator that you've created. Try setting `deltaTime` to `0.01` and see for yourself how different the printout is from what we see above.

This is why physics in games seem to break in some of the most hilarious ways. Timing is critical. If a wild event happens between calculating motion and collisions, objects can get embedded in walls, and characters can be launched into the sky at the speed of light.

Bouncy Bouncy

Things bounce when their kinetic energy can't be transferred entirely into whatever object they hit. Instead, the energy is *returned* to the bouncy object. In a perfect world of physics, we would get 100% energy transfer, but this doesn't work in reality. The amount of energy that is transferred depends on the mass and makeup of an object, and even if *those* specs were perfect, you'd still lose energy through heat and light!

We'll make our projectile bouncy by specifying its bounciness. There are a bunch of other variables we should be setting individually to determine an object's bounciness, (mass, elasticity, etc.), but bundling them all into one makes things a little simpler. This value will tell our simulation how much energy should be returned to the projectile. So, a bounciness of 1.0 means that it should return 100% of its energy after hitting the ground. 0.9 would be 90%.

Start by adding a bounciness property to the top of the file, just under deltaTime.

```
let bounciness: Double = 0.9
```

Inside the if verticalDisplacement < 0 { } statement, delete the break, and add the following:

```
verticalVelocity = -(verticalVelocity * bounciness)
```

If the verticalDisplacement drops to zero, this statement will multiply verticalVelocity by 0.9, turn it into a negative, and set that back to the verticalVelocity. This will send the projectile back up into the air; gravity will take over eventually and send it back down. This process will repeat, giving us a bounce effect.

To see this all working, run the playground again, click the box located within the side bar next to the verticalDisplacement += verticalVelocity * deltaTime line, and have a look at the graph (Figure 5-4).

26   `verticalDisplacement += verticalVelocity * deltaTime`

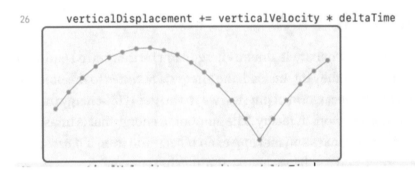

Figure 5-4. *The bounce can be seen in the verticalDisplacement graph*

The one for `verticalVelocity += gravity * deltaTime` is worth a look too. You might need to increase the number of times the while-loop executes now to see the full tail of these graphs. I set mine to 50 seconds.

Awesome right? Play around some more with the values like bounciness, gravity (remember the planets from earlier?), delta time, angle, and velocity.

Challenges

I have three for you.

1. Figure out a way to get the loop to stop after the projectile is all bounced out. Think about at what point you would consider the object to be rolling, rather than bouncing. Time between bounces? Max velocity reached? Max vertical distance traveled per bounce? Come up with a threshold.

2. Add some walls. One at the starting point and another some distance away to the right. Have the object bounce off these walls just like how it bounces off the ground.

3. Calculate the bounciness value based on the values
    of real-world objects. Things like elasticity and mass.
    You should be able to find them for a few objects like
    golf or tennis balls online. This will let you modify
    the simulation to model real-world objects. You
    can apply this thinking to calculating velocity too
    like making use of pounds per square inch. Create a
    working model for a crossbow, or paintball gun.

Summary

There's a bit to unpack from this chapter. Besides simulating projectiles
flying across an Earth-like planet, we also learned some valuable lessons
about trusting the results we get from such simulations.

In the real world we would run them many times, with different
conditions, and compare the answers to more established and trusted
sources. There are also times where we don't have pre-established ideas
about how certain systems should work, and so simulations are all we
have. The Three-Body Problem is one such example of a problem with no
solution, but can be modeled with simulations.

You learned about how while-loops work in Swift, a few handy little
math functions, and why delta time is such an important tool.

In the next chapter I'll teach you how to draw your simulations using
colors and shapes so that we don't have to keep relying on generated
graphs and print statements.

CHAPTER 6

Live Views

It's time to work on something a little bit different. In this chapter we'll be taking a short break from creating simulations and introducing you to live views. You'll also get to learn how to create art with code and how to export it. If you enjoy generating artwork in this way, keep an eye out for my next book. It will lead you through creating chaotic looped animations, fractals, image filters, and terrain/planet generation.

We'll start by creating a new playground called **10Print**.

10Print goes way back to the days of BASIC. Back then one of the first things you would do when programming on your C64 computer—besides printing out "Hello, World"—would be to create this maze-like artwork.

```
10 PRINT CHR$(205.5+RND(1)); : GOTO 10
```

That single line of code would generate a block of text using a random sequence of back-slashes and forward-slashes. In this chapter we'll be creating a similar pattern, and using the Swift Playgrounds Live View to display it.

10Print

Since generating art like this can be quite heavy on resources—especially at high resolutions—we're going to move most of our code into another source file. So, the first thing we need to do is create a new file inside the sources folder and name it TenPrint.swift. We'll then create a new empty class in that file with the same name.

```
public class TenPrint {
}
```

We'll also need something to present to the live view, so let's create a view to present!

To gain access to the UIKit framework that has all the code for views, add another import statement below `import Foundation`.

```
import UIKit
```

Inside the TenPrint class, add a `UIView` as a new property and name it `view`.

```
public let view: UIView
```

You'll get an error indicating that there are no initializers.

To fix this we'll need to add one because while we have declared a view property, we haven't initialized it with a value. Trying to use this view when there's nothing there will cause a crash, and so Swift is protecting us from that by raising an error.

Let's think about what we need to pass into this initializer. Something that we may want to have control over is the size of the *canvas* for our artwork. Another parameter would be how dense we'd like the 10Print maze to be. Since 10Print is drawn in a grid, we can call this parameter `gridSize`.

Let's add both of those to the initializer.

```
public init(gridSize: Int, canvasSize: CGSize) {

}
```

We fixed the first error, but now the Swift compiler is complaining again. It's kind of the same issue though. `view` still hasn't been initialized.

Inside the init() function, create our view.

```
let origin = CGPoint(x: 0, y: 0)
let frame = CGRect(origin: origin, size: canvasSize)
view = UIView(frame: frame)
```

You know what, while we're at it, let's add a background color to the view. I'm going to make mine gray.

```
view.backgroundColor = UIColor.gray
```

Time to start drawing!

Live View

Navigate back to the main playground file. To add support to playgrounds for live view, we need to import a particular playground module called PlaygroundSupport.

```
import PlaygroundSupport
```

Surprisingly there isn't a whole lot of information in Apple's documentation about this module, but it does have some useful commentary in its definition. Comments can be accessed by holding down the command button and clicking on the module name. This opens a little menu at your cursor, and then all you have to do is click **Jump to Definition** (see Figure 6-1).

Figure 6-1. *Command-clicking module name and selecting Jump to Definition will take you to a generated header file for that module*

About halfway through this file you will find a property called liveView. Have a read of the documentation. It looks like we need to assign our view to this property. Check out a few other comments in this file; we'll be working with some of them later in the chapter.

When you're done digging around, navigate back to the main playground file and create a new instance of TenPrint.

```
let canvasSize = CGSize(width: 200, height: 200)
let tenPrint = TenPrint(gridSize: 10, canvasSize: canvasSize)
```

Then we'll assign tenPrint.view to the playgrounds liveView property.

```
PlaygroundPage.current.liveView = tenPrint.view
```

Run your playground. You should see a view pop open to the right side of the playground window with a gray box inside. If you don't see this, you can try opening up the assistant editor and changing the dropdown from Manual to Live View. Or alternatively use the keyboard shortcut option+command+enter.

Congratulations, your first piece of code-generated art. I'm calling mine Cloudy Sky!

Generating the Maze

The final 10Print maze-like image *looks* more complicated than it is. In fact, it's just a bunch of randomly generated diagonal lines in a grid. To create something like this, we can break it down into a few simple steps.

1. Flip a coin. If it's heads, draw a forward-slash, and if it's tails, draw a back-slash.

2. Repeat step 1 until canvas width is reached.

3. Move down a row.

4. Repeat steps 2 and 3 until canvas height is reached, then exit.

So much more straightforward and easier to understand once it's been broken down like this.

We're going to use UIKit's UIBezierPath to draw the lines on our canvas. You can create any shape you like with this class. The way UIBezierPath works is like a connect-the-dots puzzle. You give it instructions, one by one, adding coordinates of where you want lines to connect. Let's try this out by drawing a triangle just below where we assign the playgrounds live view.

```
let path = UIBezierPath()
path.move(to: .zero)
path.addLine(to: CGPoint(x: 0, y: 30))
path.addLine(to: CGPoint(x: 30, y: 0))
path.close()
```

We always have to start our path with a starting point, so the move function handles that. Afterward you can add as many lines or curves as you like. Have a play around with a few of the different functions if you want. At this point these won't be drawn into the canvas, but you can view the shapes as embedded results within the code by clicking on the little square in the side panel. See Figure 6-2.

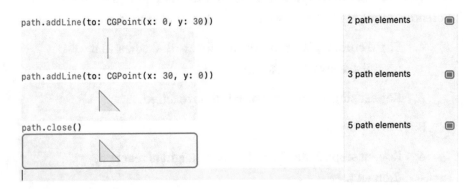

Figure 6-2. *Inline preview for each stage of a UIBezierPath triangle being drawn*

This is a very powerful feature. You can see what each function is actually doing in your path drawing code. It makes getting your head around these functions so much easier.

Let's delete that path code and navigate back to the TenPrint source file.

Within the init function we'll add some similar Bezier path code to draw our maze.

```
let path = UIBezierPath()
for y in 0..<Int(canvasSize.height) {
    for x in 0..<Int(canvasSize.width) {

    }
}
```

The first loop iterates over every point along the y-axis of our canvas' height. At each step, the inside for-loop will be run, iterating over every point in the x-axis—the width of the canvas. Following this pattern, the image will be drawn from top to bottom, left to right. We can represent this as a 2D array like so:

```
[[r0,r1,r2,r3,r4,r5], // row 0
 [r0,r1,r2,r3,r4,r5], // row 1
 [r0,r1,r2,r3,r4,r5], // row 2
 [r0,r1,r2,r3,r4,r5]] // row 3
```

There's one small problem. We don't want to draw our lines at every single point in the grid. That would fill up every space, and the result would appear as a solid color. Our lines need spaces between them. So, let's make our loops skip all points we're not interested in by adding a modulo operation. Modify the for-loops with the following:

```
for y in 0..<Int(canvasSize.height) where y % gridSize == 0 {
    for x in 0..<Int(canvasSize.width) where x % gridSize == 0
{

    }
}
```

This divides **x** and **y** by gridSize and checks that there is nothing left over. If a remainder exists, we skip to the next loop.

We do this to ensure that we draw the lines at gridSize intervals so that we can achieve a result that is similar to Figure 6-3.

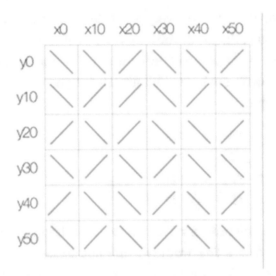

Figure 6-3. *Diagram showing even distribution of UIBezierPaths within a grid*

Inside the `canvasHeight` for-loop is where we'll perform our coin-flip to determine the orientation of the line we want to draw. We'll use `Int.random()` to perform this coin-flip.

```
if Int.random(in: 0..<2) == 0 {

} else {

}
```

Inside the if statement, we'll tell `path` to move to the bottom-left corner of a new grid square and then draw a line toward the top right.

```
path.move(to: CGPoint(x: x, y: y))
path.addLine(to: CGPoint(x: x + gridSize, y: y + gridSize))
```

The same thing goes for the else statement, except this time the path will be instructed to move to the top left of the square and draw a line toward the bottom right.

```
path.move(to: CGPoint(x: x, y: y + gridSize))
path.addLine(to: CGPoint(x: x + gridSize, y: y))
```

We're about to finish up. All we have to do now is render the path to something we can see. At the moment it's just a list of data points.

Outside both for-loops and at the bottom of the init function is where we'll handle this.

```
let layer = CAShapeLayer()
layer.strokeColor = UIColor.blue.cgColor
layer.path = path.cgPath
view.layer.addSublayer(layer)
```

CAShapeLayer is a special class that knows how to render paths. We also need to set a strokeColor; otherwise the path will be transparent when rendered. You can set this to any color you like, but I've chosen blue. We must also convert the UIColor to a cgColor and then convert the path to a cgPath. Thankfully Apple has provided an easy way for us to do this.

Go back to the main file and run your playground. You should now see your beautiful artwork.

Play around with the input parameters on the TenPrint init a little while until you find a combination that you like. Maybe you could even add a new parameter to the init() function of TenPrint.swift so that you can customize the path color.

Exporting Images

A simple process with very few lines of code. Before writing any though, you must create a new folder inside your documents folder on your Mac called **Shared Playground Data**.

This is the location that `playgroundSharedDataDirectory` points to, and it *must* exist, as Xcode will *not* create it for you. If you check the `PlaygroundSupport` documentation we looked at earlier, you'll find some more information about it there.

To perform the actual export, we're going to use something called `UIGraphicsImageRenderer` to render the view in the `TenPrint` class and convert it to a `UIImage`. Then we convert the `UIImage` to a `Data` object, which will be what we'll end up exporting. We'll add this code to the bottom of the main playground file.

```
let renderer = UIGraphicsImageRenderer(bounds: tenPrint.view.
bounds)
```

```
let image = renderer.image { rendererContext in
    tenPrint.view.layer.render(in: rendererContext.cgContext)
}
```

```
let data = image.jpegData(compressionQuality: 1.0)
```

After that we'll create a URL that points to where we'll be storing the image. I've named my image `10Print.jpg` but you can call yours whatever you like.

```
let rootUrl = playgroundSharedDataDirectory
let savePath = rootUrl.appendingPathComponent("10Print.jpg")
```

Now we export.

```
try? data?.write(to: savePath)
```

The particular function on `Data` responsible for writing to the file system can throw an error. Usually in production code we would wrap this in a do/catch statement so that we can grab the error and do something with it. Since we're only working within a playground, we'll prefix it with try?. In the case that write() *does* throw an error, there won't be any output. It will be easy to check that this has happened because our playground will fail to save the image.

Run the playground again and navigate to ~/**Documents/Shared Playground Data/**, and you should see your saved artwork—Figure 6-4!

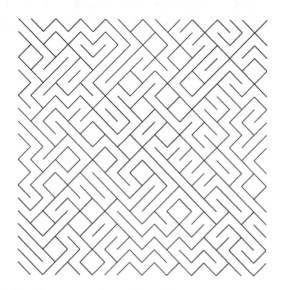

Figure 6-4. *A final exported render of the 10Print image*

Summary

While this chapter wasn't about simulations, we did get some practice with drawing Bezier paths using CAShapeLayer. This is a vital step if we are to create graphical simulations where we can watch them unfold in real time, rather than staring at a stream of text. We even discovered how to display our artwork with live views and exported them out to an image on our computer's file system.

We also had a look at 2D arrays, how they relate to grids, and how to read and manipulate the data stored in them. This will especially come in handy because the next system we're simulating is also based on a grid!

Let's also not forget the fancy little *where* clauses we added to our nested for-loops. These were super helpful in reducing the amount of code we had to write. There are still a few more Swift surprises to come.

I think we're finally ready for the big stuff, so let's get to it!

CHAPTER 7

Game of Life

Developed by John Conway in 1970, the Game of Life is a cellular-automaton, zero-player game. A game in the lightest sense as there is no user interaction beyond the initial starting conditions and neither is there an end.

The game takes place on a grid of cells. Each cell can either be alive or dead. Four simple rules govern the vitality of each cell.

1. Any live cell with fewer than two live neighbors will die.

2. Any live cell with two or three live neighbors will live on to the next generation.

3. Any live cell with more than three live neighbors will die.

4. Any dead cell with exactly three live neighbors will become a live cell.

If you're unfamiliar with the game and its rules, I highly recommend finding an online version of the game to play around with before continuing this chapter.

© Beau Nouvelle 2019
B. Nouvelle, *Simulations in Swift 5*, https://doi.org/10.1007/978-1-4842-5337-3_7

New Playground

Create a new playground and name it GameOfLife. From the preceding description of the game, you might already have an idea of the kind of elements we'll need to create. A cell and world object are a great place to start.

Let's create two new files in the sources folder of our playground and call them Cell.swift and World.swift.

We're also going to be making use of Swift Playgrounds live views like we did in the last chapter. While it might be okay to print out results to the console, being able to *see* our world come alive is even better! So, create another file and call it WorldView.swift.

Cells

Cells represent each of the little lives in the simulation. They can be in one of two states—dead or alive—they also know their position in the world. These are the properties we'll add to our cell.

Open up Cell.swift and under import Foundation create a new public enum and name it State.

```swift
public enum State {
    case alive
    case dead
}
```

Below the enum is where we will create our cell struct.

```swift
public struct Cell {
    public let x: Int
    public let y: Int
    public var state: State
}
```

Usually we would take advantage of the fact that structure gives us an initializer without doing any further work. We're using playgrounds though, and that means we need to have a public initializer to use this struct to create cells within other source files. Unfortunately, we don't get a public initializer for free, so let's add that real quick.

```
public init(x: Int, y: Int, state: State) {
    self.x = x
    self.y = y
    self.state = state
}
```

We'll also give a cell the ability to tell us if it is next to a given cell. This will help when enforcing our game rules where we determine if the cell should be dead or alive based on the state of its neighbors.

```
public func isNeighbor(to cell: Cell) -> Bool {
    let xDelta = abs(self.x - cell.x)
    let yDelta = abs(self.y - cell.y)

    switch (xDelta, yDelta) {
    case (1, 1), (0, 1), (1, 0):
        return true
    default:
        return false
    }
}
```

The calculations performed here will take the coordinates of both cells and check if they are situated right next to each other.

If one cell is at x position of 10 and the other cell is at x position of 11, (11 - 10 = 1) or (10 - 11 = -1). Wrapping the result within abs() gives us an absolute value. So, -1 becomes 1. Whether the subtraction is (10 - 11) or (11 - 10), we get the same result either way. This indicates that the cells are neighbors on the x-axis. For cells to be neighbors they cannot be any further than one point away from each other on either axis.

We can test that this works by going back to our main playground file and creating a few cells.

```
varfirstCell = Cell(x: 10, y: 10, state: .dead)
varsecondCell = Cell(x: 11, y: 11, state: .dead)
// true - Adjacent row, adjacent column.
print(firstCell.isNeighbor(to: secondCell))
```

This code will print true to the console as secondCell is one step away on both axes from firstCell. Let's try some more combinations.

```
firstCell = Cell(x: 10, y: 10, state: .dead)
secondCell = Cell(x: 11, y: 10, state: .dead)
// true - Same row, adjacent column.
print(firstCell.isNeighbor(to: secondCell))

firstCell = Cell(x: 10, y: 10, state: .dead)
secondCell = Cell(x: 20, y: 10, state: .dead)
// false - Same row, vastly different column.
print(firstCell.isNeighbor(to: secondCell))

firstCell = Cell(x: 10, y: 10, state: .dead)
secondCell = Cell(x: 10, y: 10, state: .dead)
// false - Same row, same column. They're identical!
print(firstCell.isNeighbor(to: secondCell))
```

Okay so the last one probably won't happen in our simulation, but it's worth testing out anyway.

World

The world is where our cells will live out their entire lives. It's also where we will set up most of the logic and rules for the game.

To start with, we'll need somewhere to store our cells, and we'll also need to know how many cells are required to fill the world. Open up the World.swift file and create the class.

```
public class World {
    public var cells = [Cell]()
    public let size: Int
}
```

size will be the number of cells that can fit across both axes of the world grid. A world with the size of 10 would be able to support 100 cells. Let's add an initializer to remove that pesky error.

```
public init(size: Int) {
    self.size = size
}
```

This initializer gives us an excellent entry point into this class. Being able to specify a size at initialization is important because the next step is to fill the cells array with cells.

Still inside the world initializer, add the following code:

```
for y in 0..<size {
    for x in 0..<size {
        let random = Int.random(in: 0..<3)
        let state: State = random == 0 ? .alive : .dead
        let cell = Cell(x: x, y: y, state: state)
        cells.append(cell)
    }
}
```

Much like the 10Print art playground, we have ourselves another nested array, or more commonly referred to as the 2D array. 2D arrays are used almost exclusively for building out a grid. You *can* achieve a grid with a 1D array, and we will get to that a bit later, but 2D arrays are the easiest to understand and manipulate.

You'll find these kinds of arrays in nearly every grid-type tile game. y loop for one axis, x loop for another. However, we're using the arrays a little differently than what would be considered conventional. The cells are being inserted directly into a list—a single array. This is because we've opted to have the *cells* know their position in the world, rather than having their position determined where they might be in a nested array. The benefit here is that this will be the only place in our program where you'll see this nested for-loop.

I've opted to go for a random distribution of alive and dead cells in my world as I find that random world generation is much more interesting. In many versions of the Game of Life, players can set which cells they'd like to be alive and sometimes even make changes after the game has started running.

In our version, about a third of the cells will be alive when the game starts. You can adjust this to your taste by changing the range of integers for Int.random(). The higher the number, the fewer live cells will be created.

To test this out we'll go back to the main playground file, remove the code we have there for testing Cell, and replace it with this:

```
let world = World(size: 2)
dump(world.cells)
```

Arrays and nested type objects can be difficult to read when printed to the debug console. A nicer alternative to `print()` is another statement called dump()—dump() will output the contents of an object to the console in a nicely structured and readable way.

A world with the size of two should output four cells to the debug console.

```
▽ 4 elements
▽ GameOfLife_Sources.Cell
    - x: 0
    - y: 0
    - state: GameOfLife_Sources.State.alive
▽ GameOfLife_Sources.Cell
    - x: 0
    - y: 1
    - state: GameOfLife_Sources.State.dead
▽ GameOfLife_Sources.Cell
    - x: 1
    - y: 0
    - state: GameOfLife_Sources.State.dead
▽ GameOfLife_Sources.Cell
    - x: 1
    - y: 1
    - state: GameOfLife_Sources.State.dead
```

World View

The WorldView.swift file will be a class where we put all of our drawing code. This will be a subclass of UIView and get passed into the liveView property of the playground. It's also there to look after the World object.

Open up `WorldView.swift` and import `UIKit` to the top of the file.

```
import UIKit
```

Then below that we'll create the class, subclassing UIView.

```
public class WorldView: UIView {

    var world: World = World(size: 100)
    var cellSize: Int = 10

}
```

The only two properties we'll need are the `world` and `cellSize`. The `cellSize` is what we'll use to draw each cell and calculate how large the view needs to be. This is like the `gridSize` property we used in the 10Print playground.

If each cell is 10x10 pixels and the world is a size of five, then the view would need to draw the cells on a square canvas of 50x50 pixels.

Notice that while the class has been made public, these two properties are not. We won't need to access them outside of this class, but we will need a way to set them to something else other than what we have as defaults. Unfortunately, since we're using a subclass of `UIView`, we must make use of its designated initializers. To do this, we'll create our own convenience initializer to pass in a few parameters and that will then call a designated one.

```
public convenience init(worldSize: Int, cellSize: Int) {
    let size = worldSize * cellSize
    let frame = CGRect(x: 0, y: 0, width: size, height: size)

    self.init(frame: frame)
    self.world = World(size: worldSize)
    self.cellSize = cellSize
}
```

Here we're calculating the size of the canvas based on the worldSize and cellSize parameters and creating a frame which gets passed into the views init function.

While we're here, and also have world and cellSize initialized in their declarations, we may as well use these as a default for setting up WorldView. So, let's create another convenience initializer for that too.

```
public convenience init() {
    let frame = CGRect(x: 0, y: 0, width: 1000, height: 1000)
    self.init(frame: frame)
}
```

Finally, it's time to start drawing some cells.

In the 10Print project, we made use of UIBezierPath and shape layers. Instead of going over the same content, we'll work on a different technique this time.

We're going to override UIView's draw function.

```
public override func draw(_ rect: CGRect) {

}
```

We never need to call this method directly. The view class will call draw(rect:) when the view is first displayed, or any time an event occurs that invalidates a visible part of the view. Later on we can force a drawing update indirectly by calling setNeedsDisplay.

It's important to inform you that this function should only be responsible for rendering view content. Any other code you put in here that might take a significant amount of time to execute will impact the performance of your application. I highly encourage you to have a read-through of Apple's documentation on draw(rect:).

Inside the draw method, we'll grab a reference to the current CGContext provided by Core Graphics.

```
let context = UIGraphicsGetCurrentContext()
context?.saveGState()
```

We'll be passing messages to this context and telling it what to draw for every cell that exists in the world.

```
for cell in world.cells {
    let x = cell.x * cellSize
    let y = cell.y * cellSize

    let rect = CGRect(x: x, y: y, width: cellSize, height: cellSize)

    var color = UIColor.white.cgColor
    if cell.state == .alive {
        color = UIColor.green.cgColor
    }

    context?.addRect(rect)
    context?.setFillColor(color)
    context?.fill(rect)
}
```

The position of each cell is based on the product of its coordinates and cellSize. This places them at regular intervals within the view. I've also set the color of my live cells to green, but you're free to set any color here.

Then, at the end of the draw method, we'll apply our changes by calling restoreCGState() on the context so that they're saved and can appear in the view.

```
context?.restoreGState()
```

Let's test this out and get some cells appearing in our playgrounds live view!

Go back to your main playground file and replace the code from our previous cell comparison tests with these two lines (don't forget to import PlaygroundSupport).

```
let view = WorldView(worldSize: 10, cellSize: 10)
PlaygroundPage.current.liveView = view
```

Run the playground and you should see live and dead cells randomly distributed in a 10x10 grid. Pretty cool right? See Figure 7-1.

Figure 7-1. *A 10x10 grid showing a random distribution of live and dead cells*

Game Rules

We now have cells populating the world, but they're currently frozen in time. They're born, but then nothing happens. We'll need a way to step the world forward and apply the game rules.

Go back to World.swift and create a new function called updateCells(). Inside this function we'll create a new temporary array that will hold our updated cells, along with an array of live cells.

```
public func updateCells() {
    var updatedCells = [Cell]()
    let liveCells = cells.filter { $0.state == .alive }
```

```
for cell in cells {
        // ... game rules
}

cells = updatedCells
}
```

We'll be using liveCells to find the living neighbors of each cell in the loop. Filtering out dead cells early on means that we don't have to waste resources looping over them.

Inside the for-loop we'll grab the living neighbors using the function on Cell that we wrote earlier.

```
let livingNeighbors = liveCells.filter {
    $0.isNeighbor(to: cell)
}
```

This code filters out all living cells that aren't neighbors to the current cell. After this we'll add a switch statement where we'll apply our game rules. The simplest way is to break them up into three steps—we can cover all four rules with these.

1. Any live cell with fewer than two live neighbors will die.

2. Any live cell with two or three live neighbors will live on to the next generation.

3. Any live cell with more than three live neighbors will die.

4. Any dead cell with exactly three live neighbors will become a live cell.

So, if the cell is alive and its number of live neighbors is two or three, it lives on; otherwise it dies. Let's take care of that first.

```
switch livingNeighbors.count {
case 2...3 where cell.state == .alive:
    updatedCells.append(cell)
}
```

Here we're switching on the number of live neighbors. We could also perform a switch on the state of the cell, but I wanted to show you another little trick that we can do with number ranges and switch statements.

Since the cell is already alive and there's nothing else to do, we'll just append it to the updatedCells array.

Next, we want to handle the fourth rule. If the cell is dead and has three live neighbors, it becomes alive.

```
case 3 where cell.state == .dead:
    let liveCell = Cell(x: cell.x, y: cell.y, state: .alive)
    updatedCells.append(liveCell)
```

We'll use the same coordinates and the current cell and set its state to .alive.

For every other case that these two don't cover, we want to append a dead cell to the updatedCells array. To do that, we add a default case to the switch statement.

```
default:
    let deadCell = Cell(x: cell.x, y: cell.y, state: .dead)
    updatedCells.append(deadCell)
```

The switch statement is now complete.

```
switch livingNeighbors.count {
case 2...3 where cell.state == .alive:
    updatedCells.append(cell)
```

```
case 3 where cell.state == .dead:
    let liveCell = Cell(x: cell.x, y: cell.y, state: .alive)
    updatedCells.append(liveCell)
default:
    let deadCell = Cell(x: cell.x, y: cell.y, state: .dead)
    updatedCells.append(deadCell)
}
```

I bet you didn't think it was going to be this simple. Before we can test it though, we'll need to make a slight change to the WorldView.swift file. We don't have anything triggering the updateCells function yet, so we'll need to fix that up first.

Touch Gestures

Since we're using UIKit in our playgrounds, all interactions with the live view are touch based—even if we're using a mouse. At the bottom of the WorldView class, we need to override touchesBegan() to capture a touch event sent to the live view so that we can run our updateCells() function.

```
public override func touchesBegan(_ touches: Set<UITouch>, with
event: UIEvent?) {
    world.updateCells()
    setNeedsDisplay()
}
```

Calling updateCells() will run through all of our game rule logic. Following that with a call to setNeedsDisplay() tells our view that it needs to redraw its contents, which in turn calls draw(rect:). Now it's ready to test.

Game of Life

Go back to the main playground file, and make sure that you have the live view open in the assistant editor (option+cmd+enter).

Change the world size to 100 and cell size to 5.

Click the run button.

Each time you click the live view, the game steps forward to another generation. Over a long enough timeline, the simulation will eventually settle in. You'll find that some common patterns will emerge over many games. There's a great list of them on Wikipedia if you're interested in learning more.

You should now have a thorough understanding of how you can start to think about and create cell-based simulations of your own. The next chapter will build on the lessons learned here with the Game of Life by adding new rules and expanding the number of lifeforms that can live in the world.

Bonus

Constantly clicking to see results gets boring after a while. Let's get the game running on its own.

Navigate to your WorldView.swift file and add this function at the bottom of the class:

```swift
public func autoRun() {
    DispatchQueue.main.asyncAfter(deadline: .now() + 0.2) {
        self.world.updateCells()
        self.setNeedsDisplay()
        self.autoRun()
    }
}
```

.now() is the current time, but if we want the code to pause for a moment, we can add some extra time. In this case it's 0.2 seconds. Without the pause, the code will only run as fast as your computer can execute the code.

Now go back to your main playground file and call autoRun() on view.

```
let view = WorldView(worldSize: 100, cellSize: 5)
view.autoRun()
PlaygroundPage.current.liveView = view
```

The playground will now run forever, or until you end it manually. Now you can watch your little lifeforms live and die without ever interfering. Just like a real God—just kidding.

Summary

Last chapter we introduced 2D arrays so that we could plot items in a grid. This time around we expanded on that knowledge by learning how to manipulate those grid items directly.

We learned how to search nearby grid coordinates and used Swift's powerful switch statements to write out our game logic in just a few lines of code.

Our knowledge of live views was also increased with the introduction of touch events. Allowing us to step the simulation forward with a single click of the mouse!

Take some time now going over what we've achieved here. Play around with the game rules, perhaps even adding a few of your own before moving on to the next chapter.

CHAPTER 8

The Forest: Part One

In the previous chapter, we created a world full of cells. We made it possible for them to be in one of two states—dead or alive. This time around we'll be replacing the states with types and augmenting them with some protocol-oriented programming.

We'll also be rebuilding our grid system to something that is much easier to manage. This new system will be more efficient than previous versions, allowing us to generate even larger worlds.

There is no main goal here, we're not replicating somebody else's system, so we will not worry about specific steps or rules. This simulation is ours to build in any way we choose.

While this chapter is free form, we still need to plan.

We'll be running a forest simulation and populating it with three different entities in various numbers: 50% trees, 10% woodcutters, and 2% bears. They will all be randomly placed on the grid at the start of the simulation.

Trees will grow and spread throughout the forest, woodcutters will cut down the trees, and bears will attack the woodcutters.

That's a rough plan but should be enough to get started. We'll work out the details of *how* these entities will interact with each other throughout the second half of this chapter.

© Beau Nouvelle 2019
B. Nouvelle, *Simulations in Swift 5*, https://doi.org/10.1007/978-1-4842-5337-3_8

A New Forest

Create a new playground and name it Forest. To lay the foundations, we'll create a few support files to determine the structure of the program and fill them in as we go along.

We'll definitely need a UIView subclass named ForestView.swift. Something to store our world in; we'll call that Grid.swift, and of course Forest.swift; where the bulk of the simulation's logic will be written.

Forest View

We'll begin with the easiest class to get set up. Open up ForestView.swift and fill out the file with an empty UIView implementation.

```
import Foundation
import UIKit

public class ForestView: UIView {

}
```

Then add these two properties to the top of the class.

```
var cellSize: Int = 10
var forest: Forest
```

cellSize defaults to 10, but you'll be able to change this during the custom initializer.

Previously we had the view look after the initialization of these model objects, but that's not always the best practice. In most cases, you'll want to keep views in the dark about what your application is doing underneath the UI layer. Views should only be responsible for handling user input—by passing messages to a controller—and rendering content. In our case, the main playground file is a controller, Forest is a model object, and ForestView is a view. This is called the MVC design pattern, which stands for model-view-controller. It's the most common design pattern for iOS and recommended by Apple when developing on any of their platforms. Several other design patterns also exist, another one of them being protocol-oriented programming, which we'll explore a little further on.

The custom initializer for ForestView will accept cellSize and Forest as input parameters, then apply them to the local properties we set up in the previous step.

```
public init(forest: Forest, cellSize: Int) {
    self.cellSize = cellSize
    self.forest = forest
    let size = forest.grid.size * cellSize
    let frame = CGRect(x: 0, y: 0, width: size, height: size)
    super.init(frame: frame)
}
```

You'll be presented with a few error messages, one of them indicating that the required init?(coder aDecoder:) function is missing. We'll add that in too, but we won't be using it. This initializer is more of an iOS thing.

```
required init?(coder aDecoder: NSCoder) {
    fatalError("init(coder:) has not been implemented")
}
```

The other two errors are in relation to there being no Forest type yet. Ignore these for now because we'll get to creating it soon.

Finally, we'll override draw(rect:) but we won't fill it out yet.

```
public override func draw(_ rect: CGRect) {
}
```

Grid

Switching over to the Grid file, we'll start by creating a new public struct and give it the name of Grid.

```
import Foundation
import UIKit

public struct Grid {
}
```

We'll also create a new type-alias called Coordinate above the struct declaration but below the import statements.

```
public typealias Coordinate = (x: Int, y: Int)
```

Type-aliases are used to make code more readable. Throughout our project, we'll be passing around x and y coordinates quite often. Anywhere we would use (x: Int, y: Int) as a parameter to a function, we can now substitute with Coordinate instead.

We've put the Coordinate outside any code blocks—like the struct—so that it can be accessible anywhere in our project. Coordinate could be placed in any of the files we have, but I think Grid is a suitable enough location.

Within the Grid struct add a property and name it size.

```
public let size: Int
```

The grid will be a perfect square, so we only need a single value which will perform the role for both height and width.

The initialize function for Grid will take a size parameter and apply that to its size property.

```
public init(size: Int) {
    self.size = size
}
```

We need to have a think about what other functionalities a grid would be required to have. Perhaps being able to query items at specified coordinates could be one great feature. Maybe we'd also like to check additional, nearby coordinates for any objects that could be there.

Before we can do any of that, we need a way to store these items in the grid, but we can't just store any kind of item. At least, we *shouldn't* allow for that. Woodcutters, trees, and bears don't really have a whole lot in common with each other, and then there are the subtypes of these. What if we want to have three different tree types and have them all behave like a tree? For our grid to support all of them, and any new ones we come up with, they should all *look* the same—at least to the Grid.

In some cases, a subclass would do just fine here. We could declare a new grid item type and have all our grid items inherit from that. But what happens if we then decide we want to add some unrelated functionality to only bears and woodcutters? Like maybe the ability to move, but not allow trees to have access to that code? We can't very well subclass from two different types, and writing code case by case for each time would be far too much to maintain. We'd be repeating ourselves too much. Our functions would be filled with "if bear", "if woodcutter", "if tree", etc. Of course, there's a much simpler way.

We can use something called a protocol. This is my favorite thing about Swift. Protocols are like blueprints that define functions or properties related to a specific task that any conforming type must implement. Any type that we want to store in our grid could conform to a grid-friendly protocol, and Grid will know how to handle them without ever having to know about their concrete types. To get a better understanding of this, let's create one.

Coming up with a name for such a protocol can be tricky. It has to be something that relates to a grid, but generic enough to fit with any item that you might put into the grid. Most protocol names end in able, such as Apple's Codable and Hashable protocols. I eventually settled on Plottable for this project, but I could have easily gone with Placeable or even Tileable, indicating that the item could be *plotted*, *placed*, or *tiled* in a grid.

Plottable Protocol

Let's jump out of Grid.swift for a moment and create a new source file called Protocols.swift and populate it with the following code:

```
public protocol Plottable {}
```

It's a public protocol and we're creating it with no contents. It's unlikely that we will need to add any extra functionality here, but the benefit is that should we decide to add new features to Plottable in the future, all of our other types that conform to this protocol will get them too.

To use this new protocol, let's create another type and make it conform to Plottable. Create a new file and name it Ground.swift.

```
public struct Ground: Plottable { }
```

We now have a ground object that is of type `Plottable`. We can also create other types like this too. Maybe we want a plottable tree, or plottable bears. Go back to `Grid.swift` and add a new array of `plottables` below the `size` property.

```
var plottables: [Plottable]
```

This array can hold any type that conforms to `Plottable`, and our Ground type does just that.

We'll pre-fill the grid with ground items which will be swapped out and replaced by woodcutters, trees, and bears later on. We need to add the ground objects first due to the way arrays work. Because they are ordered lists, they can only have their contents added sequentially. We want our forest to be randomly generated, so we need a pre-populated array that we can swap items in at random indexes. If we otherwise try to access these indexes without anything in them, we'll get an index out of bounds exception and the program will crash.

To pre-populate `plottables`, all we need to do is add the following line of code to the end of the `Grid` initializer:

```
plottables = Array(repeating: Ground(), count: size * size)
```

So, the initializer should now look like this:

```
public init(size: Int) {
    self.size = size
    plottables = Array(repeating: Ground(), count: size * size)
}
```

That's great, but how can we access this array if we haven't made it `public`? We don't want anything being able to modify `plottables` externally, so we'll need to create a few extra functions that can do this in a safe way indirectly.

To get an item at a particular location in the grid, we can create a
function that accepts a `Coordinate` and returns a `Plottable`. It might look
something like this: `public func item(at: Coordinate) -> Plottable;`
and then we can call it like this: `grid.item(at: myCoordinate)`. Because
we're going to be using this a lot, and it's more code than just accessing
the array directly, we'll want to make this process as easy and clean
as possible. Having something like Array's own subscript method—
`myArray[0]`—would be perfect! So, let's create a custom one for `Grid`.

This will take a coordinate, translate that to an index, and then return
the item found there. We'll also make sure that not only can we pull out a
`Plottable` at a specific `Coordinate`, but this code should also be capable of
inserting a `Plottable` at a specific `Coordinate`.

```
public subscript(coordinate: Coordinate) -> Plottable? {

}
```

Inside this subscript, we need to supply a setter and getter. Let's start
with the getter.

```
get {
    let xBounds = coordinate.x >= 0 && coordinate.x < size
    let yBounds = coordinate.y >= 0 && coordinate.y < size

    if xBounds && yBounds {
        let index = coordinate.x * size + coordinate.y
        return plottables[index]
    }
    return nil
}
```

The `if` statement checks that the coordinate passed in is within the
bounds of the grid. One thing we can do to clean this up is to move the
bounds check into another function.

Add the following just below the subscript function:

```
func isInBounds(_ coordinate: Coordinate) -> Bool {
    let xBounds = coordinate.x >= 0 && coordinate.x < size
    let yBounds = coordinate.y >= 0 && coordinate.y < size
    return xBounds && yBounds
}
```

Now we can update our getter to make use of this new function, reducing the amount of code and increasing reusability.

```
get {
    if isInBounds(coordinate) {
        let index = coordinate.x * size + coordinate.y
        return plottables[index]
    }
    return nil
}
```

We can also reuse the same bounds check in our setter.

```
set {
    if isInBounds(coordinate) {
        let index = coordinate.x * size + coordinate.y
        plottables[index] = newValue ?? Ground()
    }
}
```

This time we're grabbing the newValue—which Swift makes available to us within the setter—and inserting that into our items array. If newValue is nil, then we substitute in a new Ground object using the nil-coalescing operator—??.

Even though we return nil when the index is out of bounds in our getter, we still don't want any spots in our array to be empty, as we'll be drawing every single one of them in our view. To be safe, we'll always default to Ground.

We're going to add in one more function before we move on. This will return a random coordinate within the grid. This will help us out later when we need to populate the grid with woodcutter, trees, and bears at random locations.

```swift
public func randomCoordinate() -> Coordinate {
    let randX = Int.random(in: 0..<size)
    let randY = Int.random(in: 0..<size)
    return Coordinate(x: randX, y: randY)
}
```

This is all that our Grid struct needs to be functional. We may come back later and add a few more helper methods if we need them.

Forest

We can now move over to Forest.swift.

```swift
import Foundation

public class Forest {

    private(set) public var grid: Grid

    public init(grid: Grid) {
        self.grid = grid
        setupForest()
    }

}
```

We've made the grid property a public var that can be privately set because we're going to be modifying the grid throughout the simulation, so it needs to stay mutable, but we also don't want to allow outsiders to make changes.

Let's also create the setupForest() function that will run when our forest is initialized.

```
func setupForest() {
}
```

This is where the grid will be seeded with our forest's starting conditions. It's here where we need to make a decision about the distribution of inhabitants and what biases—if any—we may want this forest to have.

I'm going with a percentage of the overall forest size for distribution. For example, in my forest, woodcutters will take up about 5% of its capacity. I can calculate this by taking the grid.size property and dividing it by two, or perhaps more intuitively, by multiplying grid.size by itself and multiplying the result by 0.05.

In setupForest(), let's create some starting numbers for each of our inhabitants.

```
let woodcutterPopulation = grid.size / 2
let bearPopulation = grid.size / 2
let treePopulation = grid.size * grid.size / 2
```

1. Woodcutters inhabit 5% of the forest.

2. Bears inhabit 5% of the forest.

3. Trees will take up 50%.

Habitat's Inhabitants

We won't be able to populate our forest without having something to put in there. To do that, we'll need to create three new files named Woodcutter. swift, Bear.swift, and Tree.swift.

We'll make each of them a public struct and have them all conform to the Plottable protocol just like we did with Ground.

```
public struct Bear: Plottable {

}

public struct Tree: Plottable {

}

public struct Woodcutter: Plottable {

}
```

We'll be coming back to write some code for them later on.

Setup Forest

Back in Forest.swift we can start placing these items into the grid. The starting conditions should be randomized so that we don't have all our inhabitants clustered near each other. So of course, we'll need to write a function that can perform the random placement for us.

We've already done some of the work inside Grid with the random coordinate generator we created earlier, so we'll be able to utilize that here. Let's create a new function inside Forest.swift and call it randomlyPlace (plottable:count:).

```
func randomlyPlace(_ plottable: Plottable, count: Int) {
}
```

This function will take in a plottable item (bear, tree, woodcutter, etc.) and place as many as the count parameter specifies within the grid. We have prefixed the plottable parameter with an underscore _. This removes the requirement for writing in plottable: when calling the function. So instead of using randomlyPlace(plottable: Tree(), count: 10), we can use randomlyPlace(Tree(), count: 10). It makes the function a little shorter and easier to read this way. We've actually used this technique before in the isInBounds function on Grid!

Within the randomlyPlace function, we'll add a while-loop to run for as many iterations as the count parameter specifies, placing plottables all over the grid at random locations.

```
var remaining = count

while remaining > 0 {
    let coordinate = grid.randomCoordinate()
    if grid[coordinate] is Ground {
        grid[coordinate] = plottable
        remaining -= 1
    }
}
```

We've taken the count parameter and assigned it to the remaining variable. As long as this number is above zero, the while-loop will continue to execute.

Inside the loop we grab a random coordinate from the grid instance, and if the plottable item located there is of type Ground, we'll replace it with the plottable parameter passed into the function. If not, the loop continues until a suitably free spot is found.

Now this function is a little dangerous. It's possible that if you've done your math wrong and have more plottables coming in than the number of ground spots available, the while-loop will continue executing forever.

One way to protect against this is to provide another way for the loop to exit after a certain number of failed attempts have occurred. Creating a maxRetries variable and decrementing it each time a plottable fails to be placed would work okay, but you could also keep track of how many ground items are left in the grid, and once that reaches a low enough threshold, you could terminate the loop at that point.

I'm going to leave mine for now because after running this algorithm a number of times, it barely broke 100 iterations on a 10x10 grid with around 20 or so failed placement attempts on average. I can live with that.

Inside the setupForest function we can now start adding items to our forest.

```
func setupForest() {
    let woodcutterPopulation = grid.size / 2
    let bearPopulation = grid.size / 2
    let treePopulation = grid.size * grid.size / 2

    randomlyPlace(Woodcutter(), count: woodcutterPopulation)
    randomlyPlace(Tree(), count: treePopulation)
    randomlyPlace(Bear(), count: bearPopulation)
}
```

We're almost ready to start testing.

Drawing

Let's go back to the ForestView.swift file and work out how we're going to handle drawing all the different types of items in our forest.

First we'll pre-fill the draw(rect:) function with what we already know.

```
public override func draw(_ rect: CGRect) {
    let context = UIGraphicsGetCurrentContext()
    context?.saveGState()
}
```

You might remember these lines from the last chapter where we get the current CGContext so that we can send it draw commands.

This entire process is actually going to be quite simple. Similar to the 10Print project, we'll iterate through each x and y coordinate in the grid, then draw a colored square at each of these locations.

After where we get the current context, add the following code to the bottom of the draw(rect:) function:

```
for y in 0..<forest.grid.size {
    for x in 0..<forest.grid.size {
        let coordinate = Coordinate(x: x, y: y)

    }
}
```

Each object item in the forest should have a unique color so that we can tell them apart. So, let's stop here and think for a second about how we're going to do this. We *could* create several if/else statements, checking the type of each object in the grid before assigning it a color. But we want to avoid long lists of if/else statements. They make the code more difficult to read, and if we wanted to add more inhabitants to our forest, we'd need to add more statements, and it's just another place where code needs to be updated.

What if instead we were to add a color property to each of the elements in the grid?

A new protocol sounds like the ideal solution here. Any item in our grid that conforms to this protocol can be drawn to the view. Then, we would only need to do a type check for this protocol!

Drawable

Open up `Protocols.swift` and add a new one called `Drawable`. You may also need to import `UIKit` if it's not there already.

```
public protocol Drawable {
    var color: CGColor { get }
}
```

This protocol has a single property that returns a `CGColor`. We can now go back through our `Bear.swift`, `Tree.swift`, and `Woodcutter.swift` files to add conformance.

```
public struct Bear: Plottable, Drawable {
    public var color: CGColor = UIColor.green.cgColor
}
```

```
public struct Tree: Plottable, Drawable {
    public var color: CGColor = UIColor.green.cgColor
}
```

```
public struct Woodcutter: Plottable, Drawable {
    public var color: CGColor = UIColor.red.cgColor
}
```

If you find that you're getting errors or no code completion with `UIColor`, double-check that you have `UIKit` imported in these files.

We're not going to bother adding a color to Ground. This item is more of a background tile in the grid so we'll set a background color on the ForestView instead. This will also improve performance of our playground a little by not drawing every Plottable item that exists.

Open up ForestView.swift again and replace the code inside the nested x for-loop within draw(rect:) with the following:

```
let coord = Coordinate(x: x, y: y)

guard let drawableObject = forest.grid[coord] as? Drawable else
{
    continue
}

let x = coord.x * cellSize
let y = coord.y * cellSize

let origin = CGPoint(x: x, y: y)
let size = CGSize(width: cellSize, height: cellSize)
let smallRect = CGRect(origin: origin, size: size)

context?.setFillColor(drawableObject.color)
context?.fill(smallRect)
```

We start with creating a coordinate using the x and y values of the for-loops. We use this coordinate to pull out an object at particular index in the forest.grid. If it doesn't conform to Drawable, then we exit early and continue through the rest of the loop. We then calculate the size and placement for the item and ask the current context to draw it.

Notice how we don't care about the other details of the inhabitants of our forest at this stage. We don't need to know if something is a tree or a bear. All we want is the color so that we can make the item visible in the view. We've removed so much complexity by using the Drawable protocol.

To give this a test, navigate to the main playground file and replace everything in there with the following code:

```
import UIKit
import PlaygroundSupport

let grid = Grid(size: 50)
let forest = Forest(grid: grid)
let view = ForestView(forest: forest, cellSize: 10)

PlaygroundPage.current.liveView = view
```

Open up the assistant editor and set it to the playgrounds live view. Wait a moment for it to load and you should see something like Figure 8-1.

Figure 8-1. *A basic rendering of the forest simulation with trees, woodcutters, and bears*

It's a little harsh on the eyes so let's make some improvements.

Extending UIColor

UIColor gives us a few colors for free—colors such as black, brown, white, yellow, red, blue, green, and so on. We can also create our own using the UIColor(red:green:blue:alpha:) initializer. In order to use this initializer, you'll also need to know the RGB values for the color that you're trying to create.

Another, much easier way is to use Xcode's color literal feature. This allows us to use to choose our colors in a more visual way.

To get this working, you just start typing color literal, and then within the code completion popup select Color Literal (Figure 8-2), and you'll be left with a little square you can click on to show the color picker. If this doesn't work for you, there's a little code snippet further on that you can use instead.

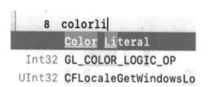

Figure 8-2. *Code completion popup with Color Literal highlighted*

Clicking the small colored square will display the color picker popup (see Figure 8-3). You can also get access to an eye dropper tool and many more color options by clicking the **other** button within this popup.

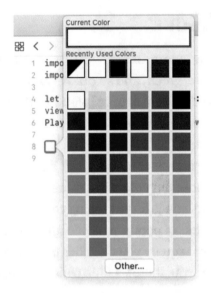

Figure 8-3. *Color Literal color picker popup*

At the moment we have three different items that can be drawn to the screen, with each of them conforming to the Drawable protocol and passing back their individual colors. Because of this, if we want to change the entire color palette, we have to navigate through three different files. Instead, we should put them in a single location to make our lives easier.

Create a new file and name it ForestColors.swift. Inside this file we'll extend UIColor with some custom colors of our own. Because UIColor is part of the UIKit frameworks, you'll need to import UIKit to avoid compile errors.

```
import UIKit

extension UIColor {
}
```

Create the extension, and then add the following code between the curly braces:

```
public static var treeColor: UIColor {
    return #colorLiteral(red: 0.3, green: 0.6, blue: 0.2, alpha: 1)
}
public static var bearColor: UIColor {
    return #colorLiteral(red: 0.4, green:0.2, blue: 0.0, alpha: 1)
}
public static var woodcutterColor: UIColor {
    return #colorLiteral(red: 0.8, green: 0, blue: 0, alpha: 1)
}
public static var groundColor: UIColor {
    return #colorLiteral(red: 0.9, green:0.9, blue: 0.8, alpha: 1)
}
```

If you want to use your own colors, then you can just use the Color Literal trick I showed you earlier and you won't need to type out the full #colorLiteral line of code.

This is the raw Color Literal code, which Xcode will format into something a little more like in Figure 8-4.

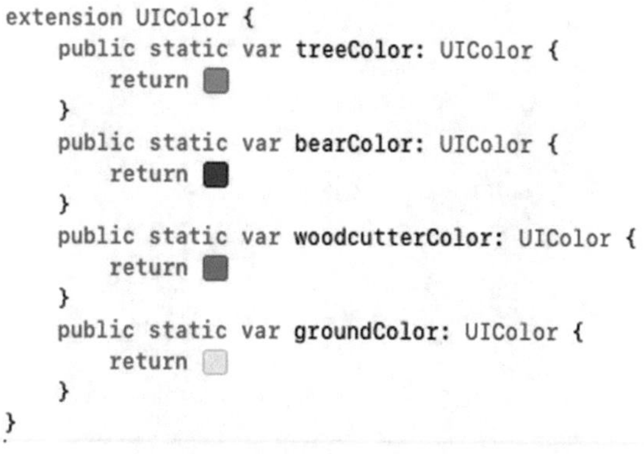

Figure 8-4. *UIColor extension with four colors created using Color Literal*

We can now update the color properties on our drawable inhabitants.

```swift
public struct Bear: Plottable, Drawable {
    public var color: CGColor = UIColor.bearColor.cgColor
}

public struct Tree: Plottable, Drawable {
    public var color: CGColor = UIColor.treeColor.cgColor
}

public struct Woodcutter: Plottable, Drawable {
    public var color: CGColor = UIColor.woodcutterColor.cgColor
}
```

As for the ground color, we can open up `ForestView.swift` and add this line of code before the closing brace of `public init()`.

```swift
backgroundColor = UIColor.groundColor
```

Run your simulation again and you should see a much more natural representation of your forest—Figure 8-5. You don't have to use these colors. You can theme your simulation any way you like. It could even be a forest on a different planet—or not a forest at all!

Figure 8-5. *Full rendering of the first stages of the forest simulation*

Summary

In this chapter we learned how to add more functionality to already existing classes such as UIColor using extensions. In fact, extensions can be added to just about anything, including enums, structs, and protocols. These are super powerful because the additions they provide are applied to all instances of that concrete type, ready to be used, anywhere within your code.

We also explored protocols, also designed to add functionality by way of conformity. Any type that conforms to Plottable can be plotted in our grid. Any type that conforms to Drawable can be drawn in our view. You can mix and match protocols anyway you like.

The next chapter is a continuation of this one, where we'll finish off the simulation with some rules for how life should operate within our forest.

CHAPTER 9

The Forest: Part Two

We now have the initial conditions of our forest completed, and so it's time to start applying some rules around life and death—you didn't think this was going to be a happy forest, did you?

We'll begin with the life cycle of each tree.

Life of a Tree

A simplified description of a tree's life cycle might be that they grow from a seed, then, once they've become mature, drop seeds of their own, spreading life around them. Our trees should behave in a similar way.

We'll make it so that they can be in one of three different stages: seedling, mature, and elder. Seedlings will be ignored by woodcutters, and elder trees will drop more wood than mature trees when harvested.

Mature and elder trees will be the only ones that can spawn more seedlings nearby.

Open up Tree.swift. At the top of the class, add a new enum called State and give it the following cases:

```
public enum State {
    case seedling
    case mature
    case elder
}
```

© Beau Nouvelle 2019
B. Nouvelle, *Simulations in Swift 5*, https://doi.org/10.1007/978-1-4842-5337-3_9

It makes sense that the state of the tree's current life cycle will depend on its age, so we'll need to add an age property and one for its state.

```
public let state: State
public let age: Int
```

This particular simulation will run on a monthly cycle, and so for my forest, I'm going to set the rules so that at 18 months a seedling becomes a mature tree, and a mature tree becomes an elder tree at 180 months. You can adjust these rules and add even more tree states if you prefer. The more customizations you make, the more alive your forest will become.

Since we've added these new properties, we'll also need to create an initializer for our Tree. When we set up the initial starting conditions inside Forest.swift, we are creating an instance of Tree using the provided initializer Tree(), so to preserve that, let's fill it out with some default values.

```
public init() {
    self.state = .mature
    self.age = 18
}
```

There's no reason why we couldn't have random starting conditions for each tree. A random age and state would make the forest generation much more interesting, but for simplicity, I've set all trees to start out as mature.

We also need to create another initializer for Tree that accepts a state and age parameters. This will be used when spawning new seedlings and adjusting the tree's maturity.

```
public init(state: State, age: Int) {
    self.state = state
    self.age = age
}
```

Let's take this one step further. Instead of having the two initializers, we'll remove the first and adjust the second with some default values.

```
public init(state: State = .mature, age: Int = 18) {
    self.state = state
    self.age = age
}
```

Inserting default values within the function's declaration allows us to initialize a new tree without having to pass in any values at all!

For example, initializing a tree by just using Tree(), without any parameters being passed in, will give us a tree that is in a mature state at 18 months of age. On the other hand, passing in parameters will override the defaults, and the initializer will end up using those instead.

Another thing we need to do is come up with different colors for each stage of growth a tree is in; this will help us tell them apart when running the simulation. Navigate back to ForestColors.swift and replace treeColor with three new ones.

```
public static var seedlingColor: UIColor {
    return #colorLiteral(red: 0.4, green: 0.7, blue: 0.5,
    alpha: 1)
}
public static var matureTreeColor: UIColor {
    return #colorLiteral(red: 0.3, green: 0.6, blue: 0.2,
    alpha: 1)
}
public static var elderTreeColor: UIColor {
    return #colorLiteral(red: 0.2, green: 0.4, blue: 0.1,
    alpha: 1)
}
```

```
extension UIColor {
    public static var seedlingColor: UIColor {
        return 🔲
    }
    public static var matureTreeColor: UIColor {
        return 🔲
    }
    public static var elderTreeColor: UIColor {
        return 🔲
    }
}
```

We can now go back to where we have made use of Drawables color variable inside Tree.swift and replace them with a calculated variable instead, passing back the correct color for each state.

```
public var color: CGColor {
    switch state {
    case .seedling:
        return UIColor.seedlingColor.cgColor
    case .mature:
        return UIColor.matureTreeColor.cgColor
    case .elder:
        return UIColor.elderTreeColor.cgColor
    }
}
```

In addition to this we can use the same formula for determining seedling spawn chances for each stage of growth.

```
var seedlingSpawnChance: Float {
        switch state {
        case .seedling:
            return 0
        case .mature:
            return 0.1
```

```
    case .elder:
        return 0.2
    }
}
```

Then, to make things even easier, we'll add a nice little helper method that will give us a simple true or false result if spawning was successful.

```
public var shouldSpawnSeedling: Bool {
    let randomSpawn = Float.random(in: 0..<1.0)
    if randomSpawn < seedlingSpawnChance {
        return true
    }
    return false
}
```

Let's add one more property while we're here, and then we'll be finished with Tree.swift.

```
public var wood: Int {
    switch state {
    case .seedling:
        return 0
    case .mature:
        return 1
    case .elder:
        return 2
    }
}
```

We'll use this to determine how much wood a woodcutter collects when they harvest a tree. As explained before, woodcutters will ignore seedlings, so there's no reason to return anything there.

Growing Trees

To test out the different colors and spawn rates for each tree state, we'll need to make some changes to our Forest.swift and Grid.swift files.

We'll begin with Grid.swift and create a function that returns a random coordinate near any coordinate passed in. This will be used to grab a spot close to a given tree and spawn a seedling there.

```swift
public func randCoordinate(near coord: Coordinate) ->
Coordinate {
    let randDX = Int.random(in: -1..<2)
    let randDY = Int.random(in: -1..<2)

    let newX = coord.x + randDX
    let newY = coord.y + randDY
    let newCoord = Coordinate(x: newX, y: newY)

    guard newCoord != coord else {
        return randCoordinate(near: coord)
    }
    guard self[newCoord] != nil else {
        return randCoordinate(near: coord)
    }

    return newCoord
}
```

If the random coordinate is the same as the one passed in, we recursively attempt to find another. Likewise, if the item at the generated coordinate is nil, then we know that generated coordinate is out of bounds of the grid, and again, we recursively search for another.

We can also use this to find nearby *empty* spaces too by creating another function that searches for neighbors of type Ground.

```
public func randGroundCoord(near coord: Coordinate) ->
Coordinate? {
    var maxRetries = 3

    while maxRetries > 0 {
        let rand = randCoordinate(near: coord)
        if self[rand] is Ground {
            return rand
        }
        maxRetries -= 1
    }

    return nil
}
```

We need to apply a limit to the number of attempts to find a nearby empty space; otherwise any item that's completely surrounded will cause the while-loop to run forever. I've chosen to set maxRetries to three, but you can increase this if you're finding that it's not enough.

That's it for Grid.swift, we don't need to make any more changes here.

We can now add a new feature to Forest that will spawn new seedlings near trees by using these new functions we added to Grid. So, open up Forest.swift and write this code before the closing brace at the end of the file.

```
func spawnSeedling(near coord: Coordinate) {
    if let validNeighbor = grid.randGroundCoord(near:  coord) {
        grid[validNeighbor] = Tree(state: .seedling, age: 0)
    }
}
```

Now all we need to do is find a place to call this function. We'll be running it for every single tree object in the forest. So we're going to need a new update function to handle all of this.

```
public func update() {
    for y in 0..<grid.size {
        for x in 0..<grid.size {
            let coordinate = Coordinate(x: x, y: y)
            if grid[coordinate] is Ground {
                continue
            }
            if let tree = grid[coordinate] as? Tree {
                update(tree: tree, at: coordinate)
            }
        }
    }
}
```

Here we loop through all possible coordinates within the grid and create a new Coordinate for each one. We then check to see if the item found at that coordinate is of type Ground, and if it is, we skip it.

Afterward we check to see if a tree can be found at that location. If this condition evaluates to true, we call the updateTree() function. We haven't written this function yet, so to keep the compiler happy, let's do that now.

```
func update(tree: Tree, at coordinate: Coordinate) {

}
```

Inside this function we'll store the trees' age and state temporarily so that their values can be updated and passed into the initializer of a new tree.

Because the trees are value types (structs) they can't be mutated, so to change their values we need to replace them with new ones in the grid.

```
let updatedAge = tree.age + 1
var updatedState = tree.state
```

After this we perform an age check to determine if the tree is old enough to change states.

```
if updatedAge == 18 {
    updatedState = .mature
} else if updatedAge == 180 {
    updatedState = .elder
}
```

Finally, we create a new tree, spawn a seedling—if possible using the spawnSeedling() function we wrote earlier—and replace the old tree with the new one in the grid.

```
let updatedTree = Tree(state: updatedState, age: updatedAge)
if tree.shouldSpawnSeedling {
    spawnSeedling(near: coordinate)
}
grid[coordinate] = updatedTree
```

To see this all in action, let's navigate back to ForestView.swift and create a new autoRun() function:

```
public func autoRun() {
    DispatchQueue.main.asyncAfter(deadline: .now() + 0.1) {
        self.forest.update()
        self.setNeedsDisplay()
        self.autoRun()
    }
}
```

which we can then call from our main playground file.

```
import UIKit
import PlaygroundSupport

let grid = Grid(size: 50)
let forest = Forest(grid: grid)
let view = ForestView(forest: forest, cellSize: 10)
view.autoRun()

PlaygroundPage.current.liveView = view
```

Open up the live view and run your playground.

Soon enough every empty spot in the forest will be replaced by a tree, and if you wait long enough—it does take some time—they'll start to change to elder trees (Figure 9-1)!

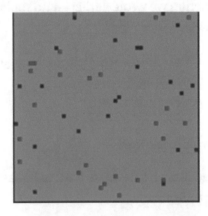

Figure 9-1. *The forest filled with elder trees with dispersed bears and woodcutters*

Moveable Protocol

It looks like we might need to breathe some life into our woodcutters to keep this forest under control! But then we might end up with a woodcutter overpopulation problem, so let's get our bears on the move too.

Both the bears and woodcutters are able to roam the forest, and they both do so with a different number of movement points. In my forest, bears can move up to six times in a single month, and the woodcutters can move up to three.

If the bears encounter a woodcutter, they will attack them and stop their movements for the rest of the month. Likewise, if the woodcutters encounter a tree, they will chop it down and stop their movement for the remainder of the month.

With both of them having this movement property in common, it makes sense to create a new protocol they can both conform to that defines a moveDistance value.

Open up Protocols.swift and add the following lines of code:

```
public protocol Moveable {
    var moveDistance: Int { get }
}
```

Then open up Bear.swift and Woodcutter.swift and have both types conform to this protocol.

```
public struct Bear: Plottable, Moveable, Drawable {
    public var moveDistance = 6
    public var color = UIColor.bearColor.cgColor
}
public struct Woodcutter: Plottable, Moveable, Drawable {
    public var moveDistance = 3
    public var color = UIColor.woodcutterColor.cgColor
}
```

Now let's go back to Forest.swift and create an update function for these movable objects.

```
func update(moveable: Moveable, at coord: Coordinate) {
    var moveDistance = moveable.moveDistance
    var finalLocation = coord
    while moveDistance > 0 {
        // Code in here.
    }
    if finalLocation != coord {
        grid[finalLocation] = grid[coord]
        grid[coord] = Ground()
    }
}
```

In this function we create a new variable based on the distance a moveable object can move and use that as the condition of a while-loop. We also have a finalLocation variable. Because our moveable objects can move multiple times, we'll need a way to keep track of each new location they move to.

At the end of the function, we move the Moveable to its finalLocation and clear its previous location in the grid. If we don't replace the previous location with a Ground object, we'll end up with duplicates.

The first thing we need to do inside the while-loop is grab a random neighbor and check that the area at that location is clear.

```
let randNeighbor = grid.randCoordinate(near: finalLocation)
moveDistance -= 1

if grid[randNeighbor] is Ground {
    finalLocation = randNeighbor
    continue
}
```

So if the random neighbor is of a Ground type, our Moveable can move into that position. We update the moveDistance and finalLocation with that coordinate and continue the while-loop.

Next, if our Moveable object is a Woodcutter and randNeighbor just so happens to be a Tree, we have to give the Woodcutter the ability to chop it down.

```
if moveable is Woodcutter {
    guard let tree = grid[randNeighbor] as? Tree else { continue }
    guard tree.state != .seedling else { continue }

    finalLocation = randNeighbor
    woodCollected += tree.wood
    break
}
```

For starters, the tree must be at a maturity level that the woodcutter will be interested in. If that's the case, all we do is move the woodcutter into the tree's position. The tree will be replaced by the woodcutter. The while-loop is then broken, since once a tree has been chopped down, the woodcutter is done moving for the month.

We're also going to be keeping track of how much wood has been collected each month by all woodcutters. We'll use this figure to make some additional rule changes a bit later. For now though, let's add a new property to the top of the class for keeping track of this.

```
var woodCollected = 0
```

We'll do something similar for when a bear stumbles across a woodcutter.

```
if moveable is Bear {
    guard grid[randNeighbor] is Woodcutter else { continue }
```

```
    woodcutterPopulation -= 1
    bearAttacks += 1
    finalLocation = randNeighbor
    break
}
```

We'll also add two new properties to the top of the class for tracking.

```
var bearAttacks = 0
var woodcutterPopulation = 0
```

Now that we're keeping track of the woodcutter population more globally, we'll need to remove the let keyword from woodcutterPopulation inside the setupForest() function.

```
woodcutterPopulation = grid.size / 2
let bearPopulation = grid.size / 2
let treePopulation = grid.size * grid.size / 2
```

Finally, if none of the preceding conditions are met, like in the case where a bear may be surrounded by trees, we need to break out of the while-loop to protect against having it execute forever. So, add a break just before the closing curly brace of the while-loop.

Before we can test, we need to call this function. Inside the main update() method of Forest.swift, put this code inside the x for-loop, just after the tree update code.

```
if let moveable = grid[coordinate] as? Moveable {
    update(moveable: moveable, at: coordinate)
}
```

Go back to your main playground file and give it a test run. See Figure 9-2.

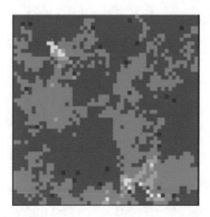

Figure 9-2. *Woodcutters are moving through the forest, chopping down trees and leaving an empty path behind them*

You'll find that it won't be too long before our woodcutters are all eaten by bears and their population is reduced to zero. The forest will then take over. We need to introduce a new rule that can boost the population of the woodcutters. Perhaps if the woodcutters are profitable, that is, the amount of wood collected per year is greater than the woodcutter population, the company will employ more. This should be enough to keep the forest in equilibrium.

Balance

We're going to add some more properties to the Forest class that will help us keep track of the changes our forest is going through. These will also help us to enforce some new balancing rules.

If we're applying some rules to yearly events, then we need to keep track of time passing, so let's add two new properties to the top of the Forest class.

```
var month = 0
var year = 0
```

At the bottom of the update() function, let's increment month by 1. Once we reach 12, we'll reset and increment year by 1.

```
month += 1
if month == 12 {
    year += 1
    month = 0
}
```

Still within the if statement, the next step is to compare the variable woodCollected to woodcutterPopulation and make the appropriate adjustments to the woodcutter population.

```
if woodCollected > woodcutterPopulation {
    let surplus = woodCollected - woodcutterPopulation
    let numberToHire = surplus / 10
    woodcutterPopulation += numberToHire
    randomlyPlace(Woodcutter(), count: numberToHire)
}

print("-------------------")
print("Year", year)
print("-------------------")
print("Bear Attacks", bearAttacks)
print("Wood Collected", woodCollected)
print("Working woodcutters", woodcutterPopulation)
print("")

woodCollected = 0
bearAttacks = 0
```

So, if the woodCollected is larger than the woodcutterPopulation, we'll calculate the number of new woodcutters we need to hire and add them to the forest. We've done this by taking the surplus, dividing that by ten, and sending it through to the randomlyPlace() function to add those new woodcutters to the grid.

If our surplus is 100, then we add 10 more woodcutters to the forest. That gives us one new woodcutter for every ten pieces of wood collected.

At the end of the year, we reset the woodCollected to zero.

We've also added some nicely formatted logging so that we can see what our forest's stats are at the end of each year.

Go back to your main playground file, open up the live view in the assistant editor, and run it again. See Figure 9-3.

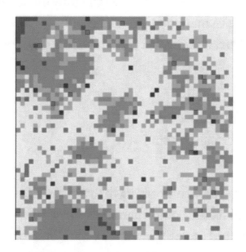

Figure 9-3. *The completed forest simulation. Trees, bears, and woodcutters living in harmony*

Your forest simulation is now complete. Watch as the bears take down woodcutters, look on in horror at the destructive force of deforestation, and gaze in the wonder at Mother Nature's ability to fight back—spreading trees out in all directions to fill the grassy plains!

Use the skills you've learned here to continue adding to this ecological marvel. Create life and death cycles for the bears, or add more growth stages to the trees. Design impassable lakes and rivers, or large mountain ranges. Add more wild animals to distract the bears from the woodcutters. There's no limit to what you can create.

Bonus

Okay, so technically the simulation is finished, but I think we can go one step further. Little colored squares on a grid look okay, but it would be even better if we could see that a bear is a bear and a tree is a tree.

We need some images to *really* make it pop!

Rather than design our own, or trawl the Internet for some textures, we'll use what we have on hand instead. Emoji!

Open up the `Protocols.swift` file, and add a new `emoji` property to `Drawable`.

```
public protocol Drawable {
    var color: CGColor { get }
    var emoji: String { get }
}
```

Any type that you had conforming to `Drawable` will now be broken. So, let's go through and fix the conformance for these structs.

In `Bear.swift`, add the `emoji` property and set it to the bear.

```
public var emoji: String = "🐻"
```

We'll do the same thing for the woodcutter. The only appropriate emoji I could find for this one was the fire person holding an axe.

```
public var emoji: String = "🧑‍🚒"
```

For Tree.swift we'll need to choose an emoji for each state of growth.

```
public var emoji: String {
    switch state {
    case .seedling:
        return "🌱"
    case .mature:
        return "🌲"
    case .elder:
        return "🌳"
    }
}
```

Now all we need to do is go back to ForestView.swift and update the draw(_ rect:) method so that it can draw these new emoji to the grid.

Delete all the code after let origin = CGPoint(x: x, y: y) within the x for-loop. We no longer need to calculate sizes or apply any fill colors to squares.

At the end of the x for-loop, we'll add some code that will convert the emoji String into an NSString. This type has a neat draw function that makes it super easy to display our emoji on the grid.

```
let string = NSString(string: drawableObject.emoji)
let font = UIFont.systemFont(ofSize: CGFloat(cellSize))
string.draw(at: origin, withAttributes: [.font:font])
```

The second line creates a standard system font with a size based on the cellSize of the grid. This is perfect because it means that the images will always be the correct size, for any size of grid you choose to draw. You can use any font here; however, the emoji images will be the same for all of them.

The final line draws the emoji string to the current context using the previously declared font.

You know what? You don't even *have* to use emoji; any string will do. In fact, you could load in a custom font made from different symbols and use those instead. You could create an ASCII art simulation if you really wanted to!

That's it, we're all done and it looks amazing! See Figure 9-4.

Figure 9-4. *A completed forest simulation with colored squares replaced with emoji*

Summary

A combination of everything learned throughout this book is crystallized within this last chapter. I tried to avoid introducing you to anything new this time around—besides drawing emoji—so that we could really focus on bringing it all together by having extra practice with what we already know.

Classes, structs, protocols, enums, extensions—you not only got to build some wonderful projects along the way, but your Swift knowledge is at the point now where you can begin to dream up your own creations.

So, I'd like to say congratulations on completing your journey through simulations in Swift. I really hope that you enjoyed it. I loved writing it, and I can't wait to see what new worlds you'll create!

Index

Printed in the United States
By Bookmasters